FREEDOM FROM FEAR

D0870320

FREEDOM FROM FEAR

A GUIDE TO SAFETY, PREPAREDNESS, AND THE THREAT OF TERRORISM

GREGORY A. THOMAS

RANDOM HOUSE REFERENCE

New York · Toronto · London · Sydney · Auckland

Please address inquiries about electronic licensing of any products for use on a network, in software, or on CD-ROM to the Subsidiary Rights Department, Random House Information Group, fax 212-572-6003.

This book is available for special discounts for bulk purchases for sales promotions or premiums. Special editions, including personalized covers, excerpts of existing books, and corporate imprints, can be created in large quantities for special needs. For more information, write to Random House, Inc., Special Markets/Premium Sales, 1745 Broadway, MD 6-2, New York, NY, 10019 or e-mail specialmarkets@randomhouse.com.

Library of Congress Cataloging-in-Publication Data is available.

ISBN: 0-375-42603-5

Visit the Random House Reference Web site: www.randomwords.com

Printed in the United States of America

10 9 8 7 6 5 4 3 2 1

Contents

DEDICATION

For the many who lost their lives or had their lives forever
changed because of the terrorist attacks of September 11, 2001.

FOREWORD
The Hon. Lee H. Hamilton

Americans have learned a lot since September 11, 2001. Words like "al Qaeda" and "weapons of mass destruction" can now be heard at the local coffee shop. New security procedures are apparent everywhere from the airport terminal to the ballpark. Voters have indicated that they want to hear as much about counter-terrorism and homeland security plans as health care plans. From our foreign policy, to our federal budget, to our community board meetings, our priorities have been reset in response to that horrible morning.

In traveling around the country, I have been struck by the sense of personal vulnerability that is felt by so many Americans. Time and again, I have been approached by people filled with questions: Who is the enemy? Why do they hate us? What can our government do to keep us safe? Are we safer now than we were on 9/11?

On the 9/11 Commission, we answered this last question by saying that we are indeed safer than we were on 9/11, but we are not safe. As a country, we are still trying to figure out how America should act abroad, organize our government at home, set priorities, and defend our communities. We have taken steps to secure ourselves, but we have also learned about the resilience of a lethal enemy and ideology that continues to reinvent itself. The threat of terrorism remains the number one national security challenge to the United States, and it will remain so for years—if not decades.

The 9/11 Commission issued forty-one recommendations to make our country safer and more secure. In response, the government took some action—notably, the most dramatic reorganization of our intelligence agencies since 1947. As of this writing, though, many of our recommendations remain unfinished: for instance, the need to allocate homeland security funding on the basis of risk; the need for more reliable communications and more effective command-and-control at the site of a disaster; the need for a set of policies to reach out to the Islamic world with what we called "an agenda of opportunity"; and the urgent need to address the danger from loose nuclear materials in Russia. Yet some of our most important recommendations could not be distilled into points of policy, and at the top of this list would be the need for public awareness.

What do I mean by public awareness? Certainly, we must learn more about terrorism, America's role in the world, and the complex relationship between the U.S. and the Islamic world. But public awareness can also start closer to home, far from the international or national debate. Begin by asking questions. Is your local hospital prepared to handle an anthrax attack? Are your local emergency responders equipped and prepared to handle a large-scale disaster? Is the food supply at your local market susceptible to sabotage? Is the chemical plant on the edge of town secure? Do you and your family have a plan of action in the event of a catastrophe?

Asking these questions does not make you a doomsayer. On the contrary, your efforts can have complementary benefits even if you never face the tragedy of a terrorist attack. If you take action on the questions I posed above, you could bolster your public health system, improve the capabilities of your local emergency responders, protect the food you purchase and eat from contamination, better secure your dangerous infrastructure, and make you and your family safer.

Indeed, Hurricane Katrina has demonstrated that preparedness is about more than terrorism. As a nation, we must be vigilant in preparing ourselves and our communities to prevent and respond to the multitude of disasters that might come. Of course, in a representative democracy, we count on our elected leaders to serve and protect our interests. But government works best when it reflects the will of an informed and engaged public. And in the event of an emergency—terrorist or otherwise—it is our citizens who will be on the front lines.

For some Americans, though, it can prove hard to find practical answers to the multitude of questions that they have about terrorism and preparedness. That is why it is so important that Gregory Thomas has written this citizen's guide to the challenges of the post-9/11 world. From the government's response to terrorism to the things you can do to keep your schools, household, and family safe, *Freedom From Fear* represents Thomas' breadth of research and expertise on preparedness. By shining light instead of adding heat to the national dialogue on terrorism, this book performs a great public service.

We are all adapting to new forms of risk since 9/11. Finding our way through these challenges will be tough. Success depends upon a vigorous and informed dialogue that is in this nation's great tradition—a dialogue that taps the idealism, innovation, and toughness of the American people, so that our citizens and our nation can move closer to the realization of President Roosevelt's fourth freedom: the freedom from fear. Put me down on the side of the optimists.

We look forward to a world
founded upon four essential human
freedoms. The first is freedom of
speech and expression—everywhere in
the world. The second is freedom
of every person to worship
God in his own way—everywhere
in the world. The third is freedom from
want . . . everywhere in the world. The
fourth is freedom from fear . . .
anywhere in the world.

—*President Franklin D. Roosevelt,*

"Four Freedoms" speech, January 6, 1941

INTRODUCTION

After the terrorist attacks of September 11, 2001, the threat to freedom—life as we know it—became a national concern. On that fateful day, in the World Trade Center complex in lower Manhattan, on a barren field in Western Pennsylvania, and in the Pentagon—the recognized symbol of U.S. military defense—nearly four thousand innocent people died and scores of others were injured while going about their daily business.

Even years after the attack, one essential freedom that many Americans have been unable to preserve is what President Roosevelt, in his historic 1941 state of the union address, called the "freedom from fear." Knowing that a perfect plan for homeland security is unrealistic, many Americans fear that it is just a matter of time before another terrorist attack occurs on American soil.

So far, we have been fortunate not to have suffered another act of terrorism in the United States. But we have perhaps been close. The terrorists who carried out the 9/11 attacks have demonstrated a steely resolve to cause us harm. Videotaped messages from Osama bin Laden have warned of plans to carry out subsequent attacks against our country. Disturbing information has also been obtained during arrests of key al Qaeda members and through seizures of materials during raids.

One major finding late in 2004 was that terrorists planned to target and bomb key financial centers in New York, New Jersey, and Washington, D.C. Officials in the Department of Homeland Security were forced to raise the terrorist threat level to orange—indicating a high risk of a terrorist attack—for the regional areas that were targeted. In April 2005, the United States indicted three men, one of whom is allegedly an al Qaeda operative, and charged them with conspiracy to use weapons of mass destruction, conspiracy to provide and conceal material support and resources, and conspiracy to damage and destroy buildings used in interstate and foreign commerce. The charges were related to allegations that, in 2000 and 2001, these men conducted detailed surveillances of targeted financial buildings with the intention of using explosive materials to cause serious harm.

In 2005, law enforcement officials in New York revealed a connection between the March 2004 al Qaeda–assisted bombing of a commuter train station in Madrid—an attack that killed 191 people and injured thousands more—and possible plans to target Grand Central terminal in New York City's midtown Manhattan. A very basic schematic of a building that was thought to be Vanderbilt Hall, a large waiting room in Grand Central terminal, was found on a computer in the home of a suspect in the Madrid train bombings. While officials in New York and in Washington, D.C., disclosed the seizure, they were careful to note that the sketch was not part of a larger operational plan, and that the seizure should not be a seen as a cause for concern.

Nevertheless, the threat of terrorism in our transportation system reared its ugly head again on the morning of July 7, 2005, when four bombs detonated in London's Underground subway system. Three of the bombs exploded within seconds of each other on trains carrying hundreds of rush hour commuters. A fourth bomb exploded on a double-decker bus close to an hour later. A total of fifty-six people were killed in these attacks, including the four people suspected of detonating the bombs.

These acts of terrorism forced officials in the United States to take a concerted look at the country's mass transportation systems. Newly appointed Department of Homeland Security Secretary Michael Chertoff immediately asked officials to increase their security presence and citizens to become more vigilant. While much of the response across the country involved an increase of police or National Guard presence at bus, subway, and train stations, New York City Police Department officials took their response a few steps further by administering random searches of the approximately 5 million daily subway and bus commuters. Experts estimate that this periodic increase of police patrols and surveillance comes at a cost of millions to the budgets of police and mass transit agencies.

In the meantime, homeland security officials believe that members of the al Qaeda network are conceiving many more plans, and that these plans will take a lot of hard work and perhaps luck for U.S. intelligence to uncover. We also know that al Qaeda is patient, known for carrying out its attacks years after conducting surveillance of its targets.

THE "NEW NORMAL"

Just four short years after 9/11, and despite an abundance of reminders from local, state, and federal officials, many of us still lack the basic supplies in our homes that would increase our chances of surviving a terrorist attack or large-scale natural disaster. A nationwide poll commissioned by the Gallup organization in March of 2004 revealed that most Americans have not taken the *basic steps* needed to withstand a terrorist attack—and, by extension, a natural disaster—in that they do not have stockpiles of water or food in their homes, or designated contact persons outside of their immediate areas with whom to communicate in the event of such emergencies. Moreover, those polled were not confident about the institutions in their community that would be responsible for responding to or assisting in response to terrorist attacks.

While local, state, and federal government officials will continue to do their best to safeguard our country from future acts of terrorism and their consequences, the reality is that these protections are limited and cannot fully protect us from *all* potential dangers. Budget constraints and competing interests will always limit resources that can be dedicated to the homeland security effort. That is why it is critical that we each take steps to prepare our "personal homelands"—our communities, our families, and our homes—from the damage that might be caused by any future act of terrorism, and the collateral damage that might be related to such an act.

■

I wrote *Freedom from Fear* to help empower and guide every American in his or her preparedness effort. This book is for mothers and fathers, aunts and uncles, and grandmothers and grandfathers who are worried about their children's ability to grow up in a world free from the dangers related to terrorism. It's for siblings who are responsible for dropping off and picking up their little brothers and sisters from school. It's for babysitters and nannies. It's for teachers and other community leaders. It's for single women and men who commute to and from work by public transportation, and who crisscross the country by plane on business trips. It's even for pet owners who care for their pets as if those pets were their children, and who would never consider leaving them behind if disaster were to strike. It's for you!

My goal here is not to raise your personal homeland security advisory level from orange to red by scaring you into a state of preparedness. Rather, my hope is that this book will serve as a wake-up call, allowing you to do two things: gather information to help you realistically assess your risk of being exposed to a potential act of terrorism; and develop a realistic, practical plan that addresses that risk, including the steps necessary to prepare for a temporary or long-term loss of critical resources such as power, food, water, or shelter.

To ensure that the messages and advice that you gather from this book are consistent, timely, relevant, and accurate, I worked closely with a small set of friends who are experts in their respective fields. At the heart of their involvement with this book was their commitment to saving lives and protecting families during a time that my friend and colleague Dr. Ronald Stephens, Director of the National School Safety Center in California, refers to as the "new normal"–the post–September 11th era.

Chapter 1, "Why Us? Why Now?", will provide you with a brief historical context for the acts of terrorism leveled against the United States, and will also help you to better understand how terrorist groups like al Qaeda recruit their followers and why they (and others) have chosen to target us and our way of life. Too many of us woke up on the morning of September 11, 2001, saw the events unfolding live on television, and were baffled. For most of us, terrorism, its motives, and its consequences will never be something that we can fully understand. Nonetheless, it is unfortunately something that we must simultaneously think about, fight against, and plan for in the long term. Terrorism is a threat that should not interrupt our everyday lives, but it is a threat we should understand. After all, as Chapter 1 reveals, it will not go away anytime soon.

Chapter 2, "Fear Factors," addresses common perceptions of terrorism and how those perceptions compare to reality. For example, many people perceive their risk of becoming the victim of a terrorist attack while flying on an airplane to be greater than their risk of being injured or killed when driving a car—a perception that is decidedly incorrect. In this chapter I address the most common fears about terrorism, comparing the threat posed by terrorism to the threat posed by other risks we all take in our everyday lives. My hope in this chapter is to provide you with some necessary perspective; one freedom we all deserve is the freedom from unnecessary worry.

Chapter 3, "The New Normal," addresses the changes that have occurred in our everyday lives since 9/11 and provides brief examples of the steps that local, state, and federal government officials have taken to increase our levels of preparedness and our ability to respond to a terrorist attack. Included in this chapter is a brief, easy-to-understand synopsis of the USA Patriot Act, which was passed into law by Congress in October of 2001 to "strengthen and expand laws concerning the investigation and prosecution of terrorism." Since its passage, the Patriot Act has engendered a great deal of confusion and concern regarding the additional power it grants to law enforcement officials. My goal in this chapter is to allay that confusion. I have also outlined what I believe are further security changes that must be made in order to best protect our country from terrorist threats.

Chapter 4, "A Family Preparedness Plan," is perhaps the most crucial chapter in this book. It provides steps—and easy ones at that—that you and your family can take to prepare for an emergency or disaster in your home or community. It is more likely that you'll be the victim of a natural disaster like a hurricane, tornado, earthquake, or fire than it is that you will be the *direct* victim of a terrorist attack. With this fact in mind, I provide you with recommendations and information from community and government resources to increase the chances that your family will be prepared in the event of an emergency—*any* emergency. This chapter also provides you with a road map to preparedness, including tips on which disasters you should prepare for based on your personal and community risk assessment, and how you should prepare for them. Recommendations in this chapter take on more significance in the wake of Hurricane Katrina, which devastated the Gulf states in the summer of 2005.

Chapter 5, "A Workplace and Travel Preparedness Plan," provides instructions and tips on how to prepare for an emergency in your place of work or during your commute. It features special information on what to do if you're on a plane or in a subway car, train car, or other form of public transportation when an emergency occurs.

Chapter 6, "A School Preparedness Plan," addresses everything a parent or caregiver needs to know about safety at school and tells you what to do in the event of an emergency. Because of the events of 9/11 and other events like the Washington, D.C., sniper shootings in the fall of 2002 and the terrorist attack in 2004 on a school in Belsan, Russia, many parents have expressed concern about the current level of emergency preparedness at our nation's schools. While studies have shown that schools are the safest places for our children to be while we are at work, many parents are unaware of just how safe schools are and what schools are doing to address the new threats posed by terrorism. In this chapter I also include a helpful checklist of questions to ask your child's principal regarding the school's level of emergency preparedness.

Chapter 7, "Talking to Kids About Terrorism and Violence," provides tips on how to speak with children about terrorism and acts of war and violence, and how to recognize behavior in your children that may require professional intervention.

In Chapter 8, "Managing Stress," I urge readers to take care of themselves. The ambient stresses of the "new normal"—disturbing headlines, increased violence, news of bombings and shootings, and so on—can take their toll on us, resulting in bad health, insomnia, irritability, or escalating fear. The stressors of life aren't going to diminish, but stress can nonetheless be reduced. This chapter focuses on stress management as an important form of preparedness, and provides strategies for easing the stress and anxiety associated with living in uncertain times.

■

My experience from over twenty years in public safety and law enforcement in New York City helped me greatly as I wrote this book. From my varied positions as a criminal investigator with the New York City Department of Investigation and assistant commissioner with the New York City Fire Department (FDNY) to my current senior position with the National Center for Disaster Preparedness at Columbia University, I have learned a lot about practical ways to enhance personal and family safety.

Perhaps my most rewarding job within New York City government was serving as the executive director of the Office of School Safety for the New York City school system. During my six years in that position, I rode a roller coaster of emotions as I worked closely with parents and their families to solve complex problems that government agencies could not solve. Many of these challenges were easily managed and solved when family members and other responsible adults felt empowered and took control of their fates. I've seen many children and families succeed in ways that they never would have if their destinies had been left in the hands of others.

As you read this book, I hope that you will find yourself similarly empowered. I believe that this book will provide you with a practical and professional yet lighthearted approach that will help you put terrorism, its potential consequences, and your own understandable anxiety into perspective.

While researching this book, I spent a lot of time in bookstores and on the Internet looking for books that, like this one, were aimed at helping families through these challenging times. But I was disappointed by what I found. Many of the books I came across, for example, recommended that readers conduct reconnaissance in their neighborhoods to "unearth terrorists and terrorist activities." Others provided tips to help readers escape kidnapping or hostage situations. And others provided horrendous photos of children and adults who were contaminated by chemicals or biological agents—photos intended to help prepare families for the consequences of bioterrorist attacks.

The truth, however, is that panic about terrorism simply is not warranted. If you feel that there are unusual activities—terrorist or otherwise—occurring in your neighborhood, at your place of work, or near your child's school, you should contact your local law enforcement authorities, not set up a wiretap or undercover operation or some other extreme form of response. And while I am very sensitive to those people who have been victims of a kidnapping or have been taken hostage, the vast majority of us will not become victims of such terrible acts. Simply put, many of the preparedness books already on the market are too extreme and unrealistic in their approaches. They inspire fear in their readers, and thus render the perceived risks of terrorist attacks vastly out of proportion with the actual threat of such attacks.

My aim in this book is to increase your level of preparedness for an emergency, terrorist-related or otherwise, *without increasing your level of fear*. Being prepared is simple, affordable, necessary, and an essential condition of the freedom from fear. ∎

CHAPTER 1

WHY US? WHY NOW?

A Brief History of Terrorism

It's been said that the most fatal illusion
is the settled point of view. This is where danger
finds easy sanctuary. This is why America's
security must always be consistent
with changing times.

—*Tom Ridge,* former Homeland Security secretary

HOW MANY TIMES have you been asked the questions, *Do you remember where you were when _____ happened?* and *What were you doing when _____ happened?*

Looking back, I can fill in the blanks with a number of examples. I was too young to recall President John F. Kennedy's assassination in November 1963, but I vividly remember when Dr. Martin Luther King Jr. was assassinated in April 1968. It seems like yesterday. I recall hearing my mother scream and seeing her cup her hands over her mouth as she watched the evening news. My mother was the African-American version of Wonder Woman, a tower of strength, and I remember being shocked to see her in such a helpless and highly emotional state when Dr. King died.

For many, another unforgettable event was the tragic *Challenger* disaster that occurred in January of 1986. As millions watched their television sets in schools and workplaces, feelings of joy and patriotic pride quickly turned to feelings of shock and despair as, minutes after takeoff, the space shuttle *Challenger* exploded in midflight, instantly killing its seven crew members.

This scene was eerily repeated on February 1, 2003, when the space shuttle *Columbia* disintegrated minutes before it was due to touch down at the Kennedy Space Center in Florida. For days and weeks after the disaster, residents of Texas, Louisiana, Arkansas, and states as far west as Arizona and New Mexico reported finding charred debris from the ill-fated spacecraft.

But even the *Columbia* tragedy seems to pale in contrast to the tragedy of September 11, 2001, the worst terrorist attack ever to occur on American soil. At that time, I served as the executive director of the Office of School Safety for the New York City public schools. That morning I was at home in Brooklyn watching the early news on television. Suddenly, the newscaster who was assigned to the lower Manhattan area broke in to report that a small plane had struck the south tower of the World Trade Center (WTC). Minutes later, as the story unfolded, it became clear that the initial reports were not correct; in fact, a commercial airliner had crashed into the tower. Initially, terrorism was not suspected.

Eight schools with a combined population of more than nine thousand students were located within blocks of the towers. As the executive director of the Office of School Safety, I had to act quickly. My wife, Kim, also snapped to attention. She was then a sergeant (since promoted to lieutenant) in the New York City Police Department (NYPD) and was assigned to the Police Commissioner's office in downtown Manhattan. Kim and I dressed quickly and jumped in my official vehicle to head into Manhattan. As we raced toward the Brooklyn Bridge with our emergency lights flashing and sirens wailing, both towers were clearly in view on the sunlit skyline.

As I carefully weaved through the traffic gridlock that was beginning to develop on the bridge, I looked at Kim and our eyes welled up with tears as we watched both towers become engulfed in smoke and flames. Our tears were for our friends who worked in the towers, and for many of our colleagues and friends in New York City who we knew would soon put their lives at risk to do the job they had sworn to do: save and protect the lives of others.

After making my way through the gridlock of lower Manhattan, I dropped Kim off at police headquarters, gave her a kiss and a hug, and told her to be careful. I promised to call her when I could. I then rushed to my office in downtown Brooklyn to make sure that my staff was OK and to meet with the chancellor and my colleagues, because I knew that it was time for some serious brainstorming and decision making. What would we do to help the nine thousand students and staff that were in the eight schools closest to the WTC? Should they be evacuated, or should they be directed to stay inside their schools to avoid the danger on the outside? And what about the other 1 million students across the city? They were not in immediate danger because they were not located near the towers. But should they be evacuated so they could be reunited with their families?

As I arrived at my office, I could see the look of concern on the faces of my colleagues who had gathered in the lobby of our building. Many were worried because they personally knew someone who worked in the towers. Several of my colleagues knew a firefighter, or knew someone in their office with a son or daughter who was a firefighter, a police officer, or an emergency medical technician, or had a son or daughter who worked in the World Trade Center or its immediate area. And, of course, we were all worried about the students, teachers, and principals in the schools that were closest to the disaster.

Because subway and bus service was suspended, we knew it would be difficult for parents to get to their homes or their children's schools quickly. So Harold Levy, then the chancellor of the New York City schools, made the decision that schools throughout the city should remain open, with students staying put until a parent or an authorized caretaker came to pick them up.

Just as this decision was being made, an unforgettable image flashed across the television set in the chancellor's office. The south tower, the last one targeted by the hijackers, had collapsed. This was not supposed to happen. These buildings had been built to withstand an accidental impact from an airplane. But right there before our eyes, the tower had begun to collapse. A deafening hush came over the room. The hush got even louder when, minutes later, the north tower also collapsed.

With the collapse of the towers, communication with the principals of the schools in the area of the World Trade Center became extremely difficult, because the antennas used by cell phone carriers had been located on the roofs of the towers, and the collapse of those towers thus made cell phone communication impossible. Further complicating matters was the fact that the collapses caused fires and destroyed telephone lines that serviced the lower Manhattan area. The principals of these schools were on their own.

During this period of rapidly unfolding chaos, the principals of these WTC-area schools assumed the same role that each assumes every day in his or her school: They became the "captains of their ships," making on-the-spot decisions either to stay in their schools or evacuate. Working closely with their partners from the New York City Police Department School Safety Division, each principal made the decision to evacuate. To our credit, all nine thousand children and all staff members were evacuated without injury.

As an organization, we at the Department of Education also ensured that all of the other 1.1 million schoolchildren in New York City returned home safely to be united with their families and loved ones. We accomplished this as transportation in New York City was halted, subways, roads, and bridges were closed, and airspace over the city was shut down (except for military flights).

While I could be assured that the city's schoolchildren were secure, I had no such assurance with respect to my wife. In fact, because communication by phone was difficult, Kim and I did not speak for hours. Little did I know that minutes after I had dropped her off at police headquarters, the building had been evacuated because law enforcement officials believed that it was also at risk of becoming a target. Kim and her coworkers had been directed to the disaster scene to assist with crowd control and evacuation.

It was 3:30 P.M., fully six hours after I had dropped her off, when I found out that Kim had narrowly escaped death that day. She had been at the south tower when it collapsed, and had survived by running at full speed into a church that was located one block away.

I had one other family member to worry about that day: my little sister, Monique, who worked in the World Financial Center. Her office was located in a building that was connected to the south tower, and was damaged greatly when both towers collapsed. Thankfully, on the morning of September 11th, she was late getting my nephew Christopher to his school in Brooklyn. Because she was late getting Christopher to school, she was also late getting in to work. And being late for work meant that she was able to hear about the disaster on her way to Manhattan. Instead of experiencing the tragedy firsthand, she went home. Thank God for small miracles.

As the hours and days unfolded, Kim and I were forced to deal with the news that we had hoped we would never hear: A large number of our close friends and colleagues had been victims of the attacks. These attacks affected my family, my friends, and me in ways that can never be measured. And, as the facts about the events of September 11th came to light, I am sure that you experienced the same feelings as did I and many Americans and people across the world: shock and anger.

— WHAT HIT US?

As the events of September 11th unfolded, I wondered:

- What did the United States do to deserve this? and
- Who could be behind this blatant act of war? Who could feel so much hatred toward us that they would mount such an attack, and who would agree to perform the types of roles played by the hijackers and their associates?

Since the 9/11 attacks, much has been said in the media and by government officials about the suspected perpetrators of these acts and their motives. It is no secret that the terrorist group al Qaeda and its infamous leader, Osama bin Laden, have been singled out as the culprits responsible for these acts of terror.

I am also sure that by now you have seen or heard about the videotaped recordings made by bin Laden and his cohorts in which they brag and gloat about the attacks, even going so far as to threaten deadlier attacks in the future. In spite of the best efforts made by government officials, educators, terrorism experts, media pundits, and others to "put a face on" al Qaeda and explain why its members have such disdain for our way of living, you probably still have questions about al Qaeda's cause, its origins, and how it continues to thrive.

To help you make sense of it all, in researching this book I examined the typical traits of terrorists, the makeup of terrorist organizations, and the typical terrorist's way of life. I also researched the origins and goals of the al Qaeda terrorist organization. This first chapter presents all of this information, in the hope that it will help you better understand what drives some people to give up their livelihoods—and in some cases, their lives—for terrorist causes.

Now let's try to provide you with some answers to the questions on everyone's minds: *Why us? Why now?*

WHAT IS TERRORISM?

I think it would be helpful to begin with a definition of *terrorism*, to the extent that such a definition is possible. Prior to the September 11th terrorist attacks, we in America were fortunate not to have suffered from an act of international terrorism on our own soil. But while September 11th was the first time most of us had experienced a terrorist attack, terrorism is by no means a new phenomenon.

History shows that the oldest terrorists were first-century holy warriors who killed civilians not sympathetic to their cause, or as extreme forms of sacrifice. Modern forms of terrorism have flourished, and continue to exist in areas of the world like the Middle East and Northern Ireland.

As easy to define as a terrorist "event" might seem to be, experts still find it difficult to come up with a one-size-fits-all definition. For example, our State Department defines terrorism as "premeditated, politically motivated violence perpetrated against noncombatant targets by sub national groups or clandestine agents, usually intended to influence an audience." (I assume you'll understand what terrorism means after reading this crystal-clear definition five or so times—and after consulting a dictionary and resisting the temptation to yell out *what?*)

Looking back on acts of terrorism that have been directed at either United States interests or those of other countries, it is clear that terrorism is usually aimed at a particular group of people. Most of these acts are designed to be memorable and spectacular in order to achieve their primary goal: to use the threat or impact of violence to create political or policy changes. In his book *International Terrorism*, terrorism expert Brian Michael Jenkins puts it best when he says: "What sets terrorism apart from other violence is this: terrorism consists of acts carried out in a dramatic publicity and create[s] an atmosphere of alarm that goes far beyond the actual victims. . . . Terrorism is theatre."

Unfortunately, the September 11th attacks appear to be part of an escalating incidence of spectacularly deadly terrorist acts committed around the world since the 1990s. While many of these attacks have occurred overseas, Americans will never forget the act of domestic terrorism carried out by convicted bomber Timothy McVeigh in Oklahoma City in 1995. His conspiracy to carry out this bombing resulted in the death of 168 innocent men, women, and children at the Murrah Federal Building in downtown Oklahoma City.

Unfortunately, in addition to the use of explosives such as those used by McVeigh, terrorists have also recently resorted to the use of chemical weapons to gain attention for their causes. In 1995, for example, members of the Aum Shinrikyo cult released nerve gas into the Tokyo subway system, killing twelve people and injuring over three thousand others. This attack was believed to be the first documented use of chemical weapons by terrorists. As yet, there has been no such attack on United States soil caused by a *chemical* weapon of mass destruction; however, we have suffered through what is believed to be the first documented use of biological weapons by terrorists. This occurred in the fall of 2001, a few short weeks after the 9/11 attacks, when the biological agent anthrax was placed in the U.S. mail. These still unsolved attacks resulted in the death of five people, with many more injured because of their exposure to this toxic chemical.

Generally, researchers have found that there have been fewer attacks in recent years. When such attacks have occurred, however, they have been deadlier than those that have occurred in the past. This might be a direct result of the increase in security at airports and other transportation venues around the world—an increase enacted in response to frequent airplane hijackings that occurred in the late 1960s and early 1970s. Experts believe that this renewed focus on security probably resulted in efforts by terrorist groups to identify easier methods of attack, such as bombings of well-populated public areas. The ubiquity of round-the-clock media coverage, in turn, ensures that terrorists' efforts are broadcast around the world, over and over again—precisely what the terrorists want.

Prior to the 1990s, many terrorist groups refrained from carrying out large-scale operations that would result in mass casualties or fatalities. It was thought that these groups believed this level of violence could backfire, failing to create sympathy for their causes. As terrorism expert Brian Jenkins writes, "terrorists used to want a lot of people watching, not a lot of people dead." It appears that with the September 11th attacks, however, some terrorist groups such as al Qaeda have changed their way of thinking.

WHO ARE TERRORISTS?
AND WHY DO THEY BECOME TERRORISTS?

As a sociology major at the University of Maryland, Eastern Shore, I studied the work of eighteenth- and nineteenth-century sociologists Emile Durkheim and Charles Horton Cooley, who introduced interesting theories on human behavior, including theories on why some of us commit extreme acts for cause.

Cooley developed a theory of the "looking-glass self" to address how we see ourselves and the way this self-perception shapes our personalities. Cooley believed that all of us tend to view ourselves through the eyes of other people, even going so far as to use other people's views to define who we are. I am sure that we all did this as kids, and perhaps still do to a certain extent. The "looking-glass self," Cooley wrote, is shaped by what we call peer pressure and, especially in the case of kids, is the reason why we wear certain clothing, for example, or speak a certain way.

The looking-glass theory and its emphasis on how we are shaped by others sheds some light on our question about why the terrorists did what they did on September 11th. It makes us think about how and why the terrorists and other extremists so easily embraced beliefs that call for injuring and killing many people, and even themselves.

Terrorists, cult members, and others who commit dramatic, violent acts tend to have similar personality traits. After a number of school shootings took place around the country—at Columbine High School in Colorado on April 20, 1999, for example, where fifteen students were killed (including the two student shooters, who committed suicide) and twenty-four others were injured, and at Jonesboro High School in Arkansas on March 24, 1998, where four students and a teacher were shot and killed—the United States government decided to conduct interviews with the students who were arrested and convicted of either wounding or killing their teachers or classmates.

The interviewers hoped to explain why these students had committed these horrific acts and, if possible, to pinpoint signs that could help educators identify students likely to commit similar acts. After conducting dozens of interviews, the researchers concluded that there is *no specific profile* of a student who is more likely than another to commit these crimes. However, many of the students did provide similar accounts of their emotional states: Many said that they had reached a "boiling point" after months (and, in some cases, years) of either not being accepted by their peers, being bullied, or becoming frustrated when their cries for help were not heard by friends, families, or school administrators. Essentially, these students felt like they were on their own, with no meaningful link to the world at large.

This is where the "looking-glass self" theory comes into play: We all are shaped by how others perceive us, and we all are affected to different extents when we are not accepted by others.

Experts who study terrorist groups have found that many (though obviously not all) people who have chosen to join such groups had difficulty fitting in with social groups in their communities, at schools, or at their places of work. Many appear to come from dysfunctional family backgrounds, and willingly respond to the messages of terrorist leaders—figures who are generally charismatic, with groups of like-minded followers that offer a comfortable support system.

Some experts believe that suicide terrorists tend to fit a common profile: poor, young, and uneducated. To this assumption, Brian Jenkins of the RAND think tank responds,

This would normally have been a good bet, but the September 11 attackers were older—particularly those who clearly knew it was to be a suicide mission . . . they

had better educations and appear to have been far more sophisticated than their predecessors . . . the profile of suicide attackers now requires revision.

While there is no universal profile for terrorists, and while many of the 9/11 terrorists didn't fit the standard profile, it is known that many of the members of al Qaeda and other terrorist organizations are attracted to their groups of choice because of the close-knit family atmosphere that these groups provide. Group leaders often take on the role of father figure—a role that for some members of the group was desperately absent during their childhoods. The leaders of these groups also tend to stand out because of their persuasive personalities and, in some cases, their stature—whether physical, intellectual, or financial—in their communities.

Osama bin Laden, the leader of the al Qaeda terrorist organization, is a good example of a typical terrorist leader. Bin Laden comes from a wealthy Saudi Arabian family and received a college degree in public administration, all of which helped him acquire status in his community. He also has a high stature, literally: According to sources, he stands six feet, five inches tall.

Leaders of terrorist groups are known to demand and receive high levels of respect and obedience from their followers. And if respect does not come through natural compliance, some terrorist group leaders have been known to resort to torture or execution, both as punishment and to intimidate potentially defiant group members.

To protect their members' identities and to separate them from society at large, many terrorist groups operate from remote, secluded locations. When members of these groups are separated from their families and friends, they generally bond together as "family" and become dependent upon one another for support and guidance. Terrorist organizations have been known to provide their members with housing, money, and access to education. In fact, some terrorist groups have used education as a means of conditioning young males and familiarizing them with the groups' values and missions.

As documented by numerous intelligence organizations, terrorist schools are filled with young men and women (women are increasingly being used to commit terrorist acts because of the often-greater ease with which they can pass through security checkpoints) who receive lessons peppered with daily reminders of how their chosen enemy or enemies have had negative effects on their lives and the lives of their families. Through the combined use of schools and isolated training camps, terrorist groups can thus spread their propaganda, create the ideological foundation needed for their members to enact change, and make their followers believe that change will only come through cruel and intimidating acts of violence committed against their chosen enemies.

Often such violence comes in the form of suicide terrorism, in which the chosen terrorists are willing to commit acts that will result in their certain death on behalf of their cause. The terrorists who hijacked four commercial airliners on the morning of September 11th, for example, were willing to die—and were thus able to turn those jets into unconventional and deadly missiles. Regrettably, there has been a significant increase in the number of suicidal terrorist attacks since the early 1980s—in particular the recent attacks on the London subway and bus system. Many such attacks have occurred monthly in the Middle East, either during the conflict between Palestine and Israel or during the current United States-led conflict in Iraq.

One thing that is clear is that suicide terrorists are extremely dedicated to their leaders and to their causes. Many members of al Qaeda are said to believe that their actions—which they perceive as sacrificial acts of selflessness—will benefit them in their religious afterlives. In fact, some members of the organization are told that failure to succeed in their suicide missions will result in them not being seen as faithful and committed to the group's cause.

WHO IS OSAMA BIN LADEN?

On a number of occasions since the 9/11 attacks, and most recently in a video that was aired the weekend prior to the 2004 presidential election, Osama bin Laden—the self-proclaimed leader of the al Qaeda terrorist network—has made it clear that he and his followers are responsible for the horrendous events of September 11th.

How did this man come to power, and how did he come to dislike so intensely the United States and our way of life? Let's take a quick look at his background—how he rose to power, eventually becoming the most sought-after fugitive on the Federal Bureau of Investigation's (FBI's) Ten Most Wanted list, with a $25 million reward offered for his capture.

Believed to be in his forties with at least three wives, Osama bin Laden was born in Saudi Arabia around 1957 to a large wealthy family. He was one of fifty children, and the seventeenth of twenty sons. His father, who had many wives, made a large fortune working in the construction industry and had close ties with Saudi Arabia's most prominent oil family. Bin Laden's family fortune is difficult to estimate, but is thought to be valued at between $30 million and $300 million.

It is believed that most of Osama bin Laden's personal fortune has been used to fund terrorist activities or has been frozen by Saudi authorities. In spite of this fact, it is estimated that he still has access to his family's fortune through financing provided to him both by his relatives and by countries that continue to support his beliefs.

As a wealthy and college-educated young Saudi with a degree in public administration, bin Laden stood out in his community and easily gained a following. During his time in college, he became a member of the Muslim Brotherhood, a radical group that was committed to the establishment of an Islamic state.

WHY DOES AL QAEDA EXIST?

Historically, terrorist groups around the world have formed and grown stronger because of differences and disputes with governments, their policies, or their religious practices. The al Qaeda terrorist group, which has taken responsibility for the 9/11 attacks, is no different. The al Qaeda network is seen as a religious terrorist group because of its use of violence to further what members believe is their religious destiny. It was formed by bin Laden to rid Muslim countries of Western influences that were seen as threats to fundamentalist Islamic governments around the world. The strength of al Qaeda's mission and existence can be tracked back to 1980, when a resistance was formed to remove Soviet troops from Afghanistan.

The Soviet invasion and occupation of Afghanistan was considered by bin Laden and others to be offensive to the Islamic religion. In Afghanistan, groups banded together to train and equip so-called holy warriors (or "mujahideen") in their fight to expel the Soviet army. Volunteers from all around the Middle East came to Afghanistan to bring aid to their fellow Muslims.

It is believed that Osama bin Laden became the prime financier for the recruitment of thousands of Muslims from more than fifty countries around the world to fight this ten-year war. He even opened a guesthouse to serve as a rest stop for Arab mujahideen fighters, whose numbers had grown larger than expected. In fact, it was rapid growth in the number of mujahideen that led to the construction of numerous training camps inside Afghanistan—a fact that gave rise to the name "al Qaeda," which means "the base" in Arabic. Muslim recruits were a critical element in the defeat of Soviet forces and their eventual retreat from Afghanistan.

The forced withdrawal of the Soviet army from Afghanistan was seen as a major victory in the eyes of bin Laden and his followers. They had succeeded in defeating and removing a recognized world power from an Islamic nation. Afterwards, many of the mujahideen expressed a desire to expand their operations to aid other lesser-known Islamic struggles that were occurring around the world. As a result, many splinter groups were formed.

After the Soviet withdrawal from Afghanistan, Osama bin Laden returned to Saudi Arabia—his own birthplace and the birthplace of Islam. While there, he worked to create an organization to help the Muslim veterans of the Soviet-Afghan War. He also made it clear through public announcements that he opposed the Saudi government's policy of allowing United States troops to be stationed on Saudi soil during the Gulf War. After the Iraqi invasion of Kuwait, instead of accepting bin Laden's offer to provide an army of his followers to defend the Saudi kingdom, the Saudi government had entrusted this task to U.S. soldiers. This was seen as a significant betrayal in bin Laden's eyes, and his outspokenness on this issue was not well received by the Saudi government. As a result, bin Laden's family was forced in effect to disown him, and in 1994 bin Laden was stripped of his Saudi citizenship and expelled from the country for his anti-government activities.

Bin Laden's next stop was Sudan, an African country. Sudan's National Islamic Front, an Islamist group that had recently gained power, invited him to move his operations to their country. During the five years he spent in Sudan, bin Laden ran several companies and invested millions of dollars in the country's infrastructure by building airports and reconstructing highways. He also ran a number of clandestine camps where his followers were trained in the use of firearms, explosives, and terrorist tactics.

During bin Laden's stay in Sudan, a large number of anti-American incidents occurred around the world. Though these incidents were difficult to link directly to bin Laden or al Qaeda, and while bin Laden may not be directly responsible for them, intelligence sources nonetheless strongly believe that he sanctioned them.

For example, the Central Intelligence Agency (CIA) believes that bin Laden supplied ammunition to the rebels responsible for an attack on American troops in Mogadishu, Somalia, in 1993—an attack that was graphically chronicled in the movie *Black Hawk Down*. During this encounter, hundreds of American soldiers were ambushed in a planned attack that resulted in the death of eighteen Marines. According to an account of the attack in Yossef Bodansky's book *Bin Laden: The Man Who Declared War on America*, the massacre was the result of a well-planned, well-executed ambush by terrorist forces overseen by Osama bin Laden.

Beginning in 1992, bin Laden orchestrated the movement into Somalia of three thousand Yemeni veterans of the Soviet-Afghan War. With them came heavy weapons and terrorist equipment, including remote-controlled bombs, booby-trapped dolls, and Stinger missiles. Sources believe that bin Laden financed this attack with $3 million of his own money. According to Bodansky, this was bin Laden's attempt "to escalate the armed struggle against the United States."

As a number of terrorist attacks around the world and in the Middle East were linked to bin Laden and al Qaeda, the Sudan government became increasingly concerned about bin Laden's presence in that country. The United States mounted pressure on the Sudan government to expel him. In 1996, bin Laden and his al Qaeda operatives were forced to leave Sudan, because they were suspected of having participated in the attempted assassination of Egyptian President Hosni Mubarak while he had been visiting Ethiopia in 1994. Bin Laden however, was not left out in the cold after his expulsion from Sudan; he received several offers to house his terrorist network and its activities. He quickly returned to Afghanistan, taking advantage of such an invitation from some Afghan warlords. While there, he fostered a relationship with the Taliban, a group led by Mohammed Omar, and enjoyed its protection.

WHY BIN LADEN WAGES WAR AGAINST THE UNITED STATES

By the mid-1990s, bin Laden was calling for a global war against Americans and Jews. In February of 1998, he joined other militant Islamic leaders in issuing a fatwa, or decree, which stated in sum that "to kill Americans and allies, both civil and military, is an individual duty of every Muslim who is able, in any country until their armies . . . depart from all the lands of Islam." (It should be noted, by the way, that bin Laden does not have the religious authority to issue such a fatwa, and that most Muslims do not agree with his beliefs or subscribe to his interpretations of the Koran or Islam.)

It is believed that Osama bin Laden's disdain for our country stems from our alliances with Israel and some Muslim states, and from our presence on Saudi soil during the Gulf War. However, a videotape made by bin Laden in November of 2004 provides an additional explanation for his hatred of the United States and a justification, in his mind, for the September 11th attacks. Loosely translated, bin Laden states in this videotape that

> The events that affected my soul in a direct way started in 1982 when America permitted the Israelis to invade Lebanon and the American Sixth Fleet helped them in that. . . . [H]ouses were destroyed . . . and high rises demolished . . . ,

**rockets raining down on our home without mercy. . . . And as
I looked at those demolished towers in Lebanon, it entered
my mind that we should punish the oppressor in kind and
that we should destroy towers in America.**

The year bin Laden issued his fatwa was also the year of the first
major terrorist act that can reliably be attributed to him and his al
Qaeda network. In August of 1998, truck bombs exploded at the
United States Embassies in Nairobi, Kenya, and Tanzania, attacks
that resulted in more than three hundred deaths.

Subsequent investigations have linked these planned bombings to
al Qaeda operatives. And, in addition to these and the 9/11
attacks, bin Laden and the al Qaeda network are suspected of
carrying out or supporting the following attacks on American
interests or property:

- February 1993: the bombing of the World Trade Center in
  New York City
- October 2000: suicide bombings of the USS *Cole* that resulted
  in the death of seventeen sailors and the wounding of thirty-
  nine others
- April 2002: the explosion of a fuel tanker outside a synagogue
  in Tunisia
- October 2002: an attack on a French tanker off the coast of
  Yemen, and several spring 2002 bombings in Pakistan
- November 2002: a car bomb attack and a failed attempt to
  shoot down an Israeli jetliner with shoulder-fired missiles,
  both in Mombassa, Kenya

Al Qaeda has also been linked to the following plots that were
disrupted prior to their execution:

- 1994: an attempt to kill Pope John Paul II during his visit
  to Manila

- 1995: a plan to blow up twelve United States commercial airliners and assassinate former president Bill Clinton during his visit to the Philippines
- 1999: a plot to detonate a bomb at Los Angeles International Airport
- 2001: an attempt by "shoe bomber" Richard Reid to explode a bomb on board a commercial airliner

Intelligence experts also believe that Osama bin Laden and his al Qaeda terrorist group have provided support to insurgents who are committing suicide attacks and military offensives aimed at U.S. forces currently in Iraq. It is further believed that al Qaeda supporters and affiliates were behind the December 6, 2001, attacks on the United States consulate in Saudi Arabia, which resulted in the deaths of five consular employees. A claim of responsibility by al Qaeda–linked groups was found posted on several Web sites often used by militant Islamic groups.

THE CONTINUING THREAT AGAINST THE U.S.

What does Osama bin Laden's rise to power and the rise of the al Qaeda terrorist network mean for our immediate future and the futures of our families?

Since the attacks of September 11th, the United States has invaded Afghanistan—the last known location of Osama bin Laden and the leaders of the al Qaeda terrorist network. We have not succeeded in capturing bin Laden, though it is believed he is in exile in the mountains of Afghanistan, close to the Pakistani border. He currently tops the FBI's "most wanted terrorists" list and, judging from his release of periodic videotaped messages, appears to remain alive and in charge of his terrorist network.

While we have been fortunate to avoid another attack on our soil since the attacks of 9/11, U.S. intelligence analysts have evidence that al Qaeda continues to plot attacks in our country and against our interests abroad. Many experts believe that bin Laden's network continues to provide support to Islamic rebellions around the world, and that bin Laden himself provides motivation to Islamic extremist groups through his videotaped messages. On March 11, 2004, for example, shortly after bin Laden released a videotaped message, a terrorist attack occurred in the commuter rail system of Madrid, Spain, that resulted in the death of 191 commuters. Intelligence officials have since uncovered evidence linking the people arrested in connection with these attacks to the al Qaeda terrorist network.

We continue to make strides in our attempts to kill or capture members of the al Qaeda terrorist network, but the job is far from complete. By arresting large numbers of key al Qaeda leaders around the world, we have been able to thwart further attacks and gain critical information about how the network functions and plans to carry out its operations. It is clear, however—both from a number of congressional hearings and reports and from the findings and recommendations of the National Commission on Terrorist Attacks, popularly known as the 9-11 Commission—that a lot more needs to be done to better protect our homeland from subsequent terrorist attacks.

I believe that the best bipartisan list of recommendations for improving our homeland security can be found in the final report of the 9-11 Commission. In Section 12.3, the report recommends that we as a nation take steps to "prevent the continued growth of Islamic terrorism." Specifically, this section of the report recommends that the U.S. take steps to improve its image around the world, because worldwide support for our beliefs has waned. Recent events such as the invasion of Iraq without the full support of the United Nations—and subsequent claims regarding the torture of Iraqi detainees at the Abu Ghraib military prison—have negatively impacted our credibility, and thus our safety, around the world.

According to the 9-11 Commission Report, polls taken in Islamic countries after 9/11 revealed that Muslims were supportive of our efforts against terrorism, had a favorable view of the United States as a country, and in many cases did not support the views of Osama bin Laden and his terrorist network. Since the invasion of Iraq, however, polls show that many Muslim respondents in countries such as Morocco, Turkey, and Pakistan have unfavorable views of the United States, and feel that we invaded Iraq for economic reasons—in particular, for oil. While some world leaders and foreign policy experts believe that the United States did not bring the 9/11 attacks upon itself, many people across the world see our dominance in world politics and economics as fuel for their feelings of hatred toward our country.

No matter what the world's view of our foreign policies, or whether we choose to change these policies, it is clear that for the time being Osama bin Laden and his followers see the United States as their stated enemy. Moreover, in the short term it appears that their efforts are well funded, and that bin Laden and his followers are determined to get their message across in dramatic fashion. It thus makes sense for us to prepare ourselves and our families for potential emergencies—in ways that, in the past, we never deemed necessary.

Some Americans wonder if we will ever again be able to live our lives as we did in the days, months, and years before the September 11th attacks. Unfortunately, the answer to this question is clear: No, we cannot. The good news, however, is that preparing our families to exist in this "new reality" is not too costly, and can be achieved without undue stress. Preparing for large-scale emergencies, such as those that might occur after a terrorist attack, is easy when done in conjunction with the steps we might otherwise take to prepare our homes and communities for the effects of natural disasters. In fact, when it becomes a part of our culture, preparedness for the new reality of the post-9/11 world—the "new normal"—becomes second nature.

CHAPTER 2

FEAR FACTORS

Putting Risks into Perspective

To be alive at all involves some risk.
—*Harold Macmillan*

Knowledge is of two kinds.
We know a subject ourselves,
or we know where we can
find information on it.
—*Samuel Johnson*

AFTER THE 9/11 ATTACKS, citizens and legislators had many questions on their minds: *Are we doing the best that we can to prevent another terrorist attack? Is it safe to travel? Should I ever step into an airplane again? When might another attack happen?*

In an attempt to answer these and many other questions, many families of 9/11 victims came together to support and promote public policies aimed at preventing and responding to terrorism-related threats. Through the dedicated efforts of the families of the 9/11 victims, the National Commission on Terrorist Attacks Upon the United States (also known as the 9-11 Commission) was established in 2002. The commission was created by congressional legislation to serve as a nonpartisan vehicle for independent analysis. Part of its mandate was to "prepare a full and complete account of the circumstances surrounding the September 11, 2001 terrorist attacks, including preparedness for and the immediate response to the attacks."

WHAT THE 9-11
COMMISSION REPORT WARNS US ABOUT

The Commission released a public report on its findings in July 2004. This report, which I believe is a must-read for every American, is available in bookstores nationwide and from the Government Printing Office (see the "Resources" section at the end of this book). It presents a telling account of a landmark moment in our nation's history, developed through thorough research and extensive public hearings. The easy-to-read final report also answers a lot of important questions about the attacks and outlines a road map for our country's future with respect to terrorism, including a discussion of the likelihood of further attacks and our ability to prevent them.

According to the 9-11 Commission, the evidence (both former and current) reveals that we are a marked enemy of Osama bin Laden and his terrorist network, and that we should prepare as such:

> We learned about an enemy who is sophisticated, patient, disciplined and lethal. The enemy rallies broad support in the Arab and Muslim world by demanding redress of political grievances, but its hostility towards us and our values is limitless. . . . It makes no distinction between military and civilian targets. Collateral damage is not in its lexicon.

With this chilling revelation comes a lot of understandable anxiety. If what the experts predict is true and we are, in some estimates, days or months away from another attack, what are we to do? What kind of attack should we prepare for? Will the next attack come from the air, land, or sea? Will there be multiple attacks, or one attack similar in magnitude or scope to those of 9/11? Will we have warning that will give us time to prepare? How vulnerable are we?

As a senior manager at the National Center for Disaster Preparedness at Columbia University, I work closely with parents, students, educators, and public safety and law enforcement officials as they take steps to prepare schools for disasters or acts of terrorism. I am often faced with the difficult task of answering the questions that have been raised by the findings of the 9-11 Commission. When I speak publicly on any issue, particularly issues that relate to public safety, I believe in providing realistic answers and practical solutions. This book will be no exception. As my fifteen-year-old son would say, I "keep it real."

The information in this chapter will help you put into perspective the risks you face each day. It will help you make rational choices about which emergencies to plan for, and how; you will learn, for example, whether you *really* need to purchase that full-body chem-bio suit and oxygen mask that you saw advertised on the Internet.

WHAT ARE THE CHANCES OF ANOTHER ATTACK?

As we begin to put your risks into perspective, I am going to be honest and practical. So here goes: No matter what you read or what you hear, when it comes to *fully determining* the likelihood that you, your family, or your neighborhood will become a victim of an act of terrorism, there isn't any real science.

It is impossible to determine your chances of becoming a victim of a terrorist attack unless there is "credible, actionable intelligence"—a fancy government phrase referring, in the words of my late grandmother, to the kind of information you can "take to the bank." Credible, actionable intelligence exists only when officials know if and when a terrorist group is targeting a particular location. Without solid information, terrorist attacks in the United States are simply too rare and unpredictable to enable us to jump to conclusions. Therefore, risk experts must base their estimates on the *means* that terrorists have used against us to date—such as the hijacking of airplanes and the use of anthrax.

TO FLY OR NOT TO FLY?

Due to the events of 9/11, many people believe that being in a plane is more dangerous than being just about anywhere else. We were all stunned by the calculated, unconventional use of commercial airlines as missiles on 9/11. Even today, years after the attacks, many people I know refuse to fly, or fly only when necessary.

In addition to our hearts and minds, however, the 9/11 attacks also had a measurable effect on our nation's economy, and on the travel industry in particular. Airlines, hotels, taxicabs, and restaurants suffered significant losses in business. In fact, losses to the airline industry were so great that President George W. Bush signed into law an emergency aid package providing $5 billion in direct federal aid and $10 billion in loan guarantees to the industry, which in the days after 9/11 announced tens of thousands of employee layoffs.

Shortly after 9/11, the industry's dire straits became apparent to me firsthand. A few months after the attacks, I traveled to Washington, D.C., to serve on a select panel of school safety experts from nine nations who were gathering to develop strategies for preparing schools for the possibility of terrorist attacks. It is not unusual for me to travel to Washington, D.C., at least five times during a calendar year, though I typically travel by train—I love seeing our beautiful country from ground level rather than from forty thousand feet! Because of pressing concerns back in New York City, however, I was required to return from this trip quickly, and thus traveled home by plane.

In response to the 9/11 attacks—in which two of the hijacked planes had been destined for the Washington, D.C., area—Reagan National Airport in Washington, D.C. was a virtual fortress, with military and law enforcement personnel stationed all throughout the concourse and gate areas. Due to these upgraded security measures, I approached the gate for my shuttle flight back to New York City fully expecting to deal with long lines. To my surprise, however, I waited in line only ten minutes, and was quickly in my seat, buckled up and ready to go! Tellingly, however, my speedy transit through security was not due to the speed of airport staff in conducting searches at the gate. Rather, it was due to the fact that most seats on the airplane were empty. People simply weren't flying!

As I look back on this experience, the question arises: Based on what we know about the risks involved with certain modes of travel, is the choice of many Americans to avoid traveling by plane—both immediately after 9/11 and, in many cases, to the present day—a rational decision?

Despite their fear of flying, many people continued to travel in the days and months following 9/11; they simply chose to drive rather than fly to their destinations. But although this behavior *felt* safer to many people, statistically they were choosing a less safe mode of travel. Let's look at the facts.

A 2002 study by the National Safety Council reveals that the top-three causes of unintentional injury deaths in the United States are motor vehicles (which cause 44,000 deaths per year), poisoning (which kills 15,700), and falls (which kill 14,500). Compare these findings to those of the National Transportation Safety Board regarding airline travel in 2002. That year, out of approximately 619 million airline travelers,

- the total number of civil aviation accidents in the U.S. was 1,820;
- there were eleven serious passenger injuries; and
- there were no fatalities.

When we compare the statistics relating to driving-related injuries and fatalities with those relating to airplane crashes in 2002, it becomes clear that, statistically, airline travel is much safer than traveling by car.

What does this tell us? It tells us that our decisions are not always rational. We know from research that we fear things for reasons that are personal in nature and in most cases linked to emotion. Even though airports were more secure after 9/11 than ever before, for example, and even though the risk of being injured while driving is far greater than the risk of being injured while flying, people nonetheless choose the former over the latter. The reasons are clear: We are more afraid of large-scale, extraordinary-seeming events than of everyday ones; the idea of being in a hijacked plane is much scarier than that of being in a car accident; and while driving we feel as if we have a sense of control—or at least a greater sense of control than we would have in the event of a terrorist attack—even though that sense of control is all about perception, and not reality.

RISK PERCEPTION VS REALITY

To help put the risk of a terrorist attack into perspective, I want to examine it in the context of other risks we face in our everyday lives. My friend and colleague David Ropeik, a science journalist and the Director of Risk Communication at the Harvard University Center for Risk Analysis, examines risk perception versus reality in a recent book he coauthored with George Gray entitled *Risk! A Practical Guide for Deciding What's Really Safe and What's Really Dangerous in the World Around You.* In this book, David explains that our interpretations of various risks often differ from those of our friends and neighbors, even when we operate with the same set of facts. This highly subjective understanding of risk is known as "risk perception."

The perceived (yet inaccurate) perception that flying is riskier than driving is just one example of how "risk perception" plays out in our lives. In *Risk!*, Ropeik provides a number of additional examples of how we are sometimes irrational or inconsistent when it comes to judging risk. For example:

- Most people are less afraid of risks that are naturally occurring than those that are man-made. For example, many of us are more afraid of radiation from nuclear waste, potential nuclear attacks, or our cell phones, than we are of radiation emitted from the sun, which we know to be a far greater risk over the long-term.

- Most people are less afraid of risks with which they willfully come in contact than they are of risks over which they have no control. For example, we are often more concerned about asbestos or other hazardous materials in and around our environment—because others are responsible for creating those risks—than we are about risks we pose to our own health such as smoking.

- Most people are less afraid of known risks, if those risks provide them with benefits that they want, than they are of unknown risks. For example, people living in earthquake zones such as San Francisco or Los Angeles, or in hurricane-prone locations such as Florida, are fully aware of the likelihood that they or their loved ones will become victims of these natural disasters, but they still choose to live in these areas—because of the beautiful weather, because they find it easy to obtain work there, or for a number of other reasons that are specific to each individual.

- Most people are more afraid of risks that are local and personal than of those that are global. For example, we were less afraid of terrorism before the 9/11 attacks than we are now, because before 9/11, terrorism was something that almost always occurred overseas. After 9/11, however, the risk seemed more local and personal—even though the likelihood of terrorism remained about as low as it was before.

- We are less afraid of risks stemming from places, people, corporations, or governments that we trust than from those that we don't trust. Ropeik cites the example of a person being offered two glasses of clear liquid and being told that he or she must drink one of them. Research shows that the person is more likely to accept a glass from a person he or she trusts, like a relative or celebrity, than from a stranger—even without knowing what's in the glass! This is because accepting the glass from someone we know or trust seems less risky.

The bottom line about risk perception as it applies to terrorism is that the threat of a terrorist attack is no greater—and, in many cases, is significantly less—than the threat of harm posed by the risks we take in our everyday lives. But that doesn't mean we shouldn't prepare for the possibility of terrorism; it just means we have to keep the threat in perspective.

Fear Factors

In "'Fear Factors' in an Age of Terrorism," an article he wrote for MSNBC News shortly after the 9/11 attacks, David Ropeik offered his thoughts about the new world we live in and how we can find ways to keep the risk of terrorism in perspective.

Americans are possibly more afraid than they have ever been. Afraid enough to buy gas masks and guns, afraid enough to see the most innocuous events as sinister and threatening, even afraid enough to treat neighbors as the enemy if they don't look right. As Franklin Roosevelt said of the Depression in his first inaugural address, "the only thing we have to fear, is fear itself." So it may be useful to understand the science that explains the roots of fear. . . . Here are the risk-perception factors that help us understand why our fear right now is so high.

DREAD
What are you more afraid of: being eaten by a shark or dying of a heart attack in your sleep? Both leave you equally as dead, but one—being eaten alive—is a more dreadful way to go. Risk perception research has found that we are more afraid of risks that kill us in really awful ways than risks that lead to deaths that are more peaceful. Deaths from acts of terrorism rate high on the "Dread" scale.

AWARENESS
What risks are you aware of these days? Anthrax attack or other biological or chemical terrorism, airplane hijackings, bombings—in short, risks of terrorism. Are you aware of global climate change, or street crime, or mad cow disease? These risks haven't gone away. They just aren't on the radar screen of our daily consciousness right now. We tend, as a species, to be more afraid of risks we're more aware of. Terrorism also rates high on the "Awareness" scale.

NEW VS FAMILIAR

We have never faced this kind of terrorist threat before. It's new. Risk-perception research finds that we are much more afraid of risks that are new, and less afraid of risks once we've lived with them for a while and gotten familiar with them. Compare the paralytic effect of fear on us right now, to the way people in London and Jerusalem are living their lives. They have gotten used to the threat of terrorism, put it in perspective, and found ways to rein in their fear to something more reasonable. Or compare the moderate concern about West Nile virus in New York this past summer to the panic that gripped many New Yorkers a couple of summers back when the disease first showed up. The risk isn't gone, and people are not *un-*afraid. But they are less afraid now that they've lived with the risk long enough to put it in perspective. Like the people in London and Jerusalem, this is probably how we will adjust in the months ahead, even if occasional attacks continue.

ME VS THEM

As never before, the risk of terrorism is now real for each one of us in America. Before, it used to be something that might happen to "them," somewhere else. Even when it was Americans who were attacked, they were in embassies in Kenya and Tanzania, military housing in Saudi Arabia or on a ship in Yemen. Now, as never before, the risk is to you and me, not just "them." When we see any risk as a risk to ourselves, we are more afraid than if we see the same risk as only threatening somebody else.

CATASTROPHIC VS CHRONIC

We are also more afraid of risks that kill a lot of us, all at once in one place, than risks that kill us here and there, over time. In the next 12 months, 120 times more Americans will die of heart disease than died in the Sept. 11 attacks. But they will die here and there and everywhere, over time. Terrorist victims, or people who die in plane crashes, train crashes, mass crimes, fires or explosions, all die at once, in one place. Terrorism rates as high as possible on the "Catastrophic vs Chronic" scale.

> **UNCERTAINTY**
> Finally, our fear is being fed by the risk perception factor of "Uncertainty." We don't know what may come next, or when, or where, or even who the bad guys really are, or where they are, or whether they are among us. The more uncertain we are, say the risk-perception studies, the more afraid we are. . . .
>
> Risk perception is a matter of emotion more than rational factual analysis. We are facing a risk that is new, catastrophic, dreadful, personal, and full of uncertainty—a risk that is dominating our awareness. These powerful emotional triggers are the roots that explain why we are so afraid. They explain why behaviors that in one way seem so irrational, in another way make so much sense.
>
> (Reprinted with permission of David Ropeik)

PUT YOUR FEARS IN CONTEXT

Just about every task we perform in life has some sort of risk associated with it. We take risks when we eat or overeat. We risk injury when we engage in recreational activities like cycling, jogging, tennis, golf, or even walking. Yet we continue to do these types of activities because of the personal payoff they provide, like relieving stress or promoting healthy and fit bodies. And we take risks when we travel to and from work or school every day. No matter what our mode of travel, there is always the risk that an accident could occur.

As you read about terrorism in the newspapers or hear about it on the evening news, keep your personal risks in perspective. Continue to get the facts about the risks that you face on a day-to-day basis, whether or not they relate to potential acts of terrorism. Take whatever steps you can to avoid these risks, and prepare for their consequences if by chance they should occur. For information about how to prepare, read on: That's what the rest of this book is about.

CHAPTER 3

THE NEW NORMAL

The Patriot Act and Other Post-9/11 Changes

I fear all we have done is to awaken a sleeping
giant and fill him with a terrible resolve.
—*Japanese Admiral Yamamoto,* planner of the attack
on Pearl Harbor, December 7, 1941

We must ensure that we do not lose our way
of life in the process of defending it.
—*Pat Holt,* Christian Science Monitor, October 2, 2003

S EVERAL MONTHS AFTER 9/11 I met with an international group of school safety officials in Washington, D.C., to discuss how our countries could better prepare for acts of terrorism. When I spoke with experts from countries such as Ireland, Israel, and Turkey, I was surprised to learn that they have, in some sense, become accustomed to the threat of terrorism. Not that they think terrorism is acceptable or that they stop fighting against it—on the contrary, they have found ways to combat it while at the same time going on with their everyday lives. But for people living in these countries, the threat of terrorism is a normal (if not acceptable) part of life, posing a risk no greater than the risk posed by driving.

I wouldn't go so far as to say that, even years after 9/11, Americans have accepted the risks of terrorism to the same extent that the Irish, Israelis, and Turks have. Some of us simply deny the threat as much as possible. But it's impossible to ignore the fact that the threat of terrorism continues, and will continue, to affect our everyday lives—whether we're flying on a plane or simply checking out a library book—due in large part to legislation such as the USA Patriot Act that the government has introduced in its so-called war on terror.

But now that several years have passed since 9/11, questions still remain about our nation's current level of security and the personal, financial, and legal sacrifices that we've had to make to get us where we are. Has the money been well spent? Have the new laws trampled on our civil liberties? Are we safer as a nation?

In this chapter we will take a quick look at what I will call our "new normal": the effects of antiterrorist initiatives in our everyday lives. It will cover what our government has done—and in some cases *not* done—to make us safer and better prepared for potential terrorist attacks.

THE WAR ON TERROR

To understand the current war on terror and how it affects us today, it may be helpful to first rewind back to 9/11 and examine the immediate actions our government took against terrorist activity. In his speech to the nation on the evening of September 11th, President Bush proclaimed that

> [A] great people has been moved to defend a great nation . . . terrorist attacks can shake the foundations of our biggest buildings, but they cannot touch the foundation of America. These acts shattered steel, but they cannot dent the steel of American resolve. America was targeted for attack because we're the brightest beacon for freedom and opportunity in the world. And no one will keep that light from shining.

Within hours after the 9/11 attacks, United States intelligence officials identified Osama bin Laden as the suspect behind the attacks. With bin Laden and his supporters as clear culprits, our government took steps to bring them quickly to justice. In actions that have gone on to exemplify his first term in office, President Bush developed plans for what has been dubbed a "war on terror," in which the United States and its allies have come together to focus military, political, and economic efforts against countries or groups that support or harbor terrorists. In addition, the President sought permission from Congress to invade Afghanistan, both for the purpose of unseating the Taliban government, which was known to provide support to terrorists, and because it was the last known haunt of Osama bin Laden and his al Qaeda network. The United States sent the Taliban government a clear message: that failure to comply with U.S. demands to deliver terrorists and their supporting structures would result in military retaliation from our country and its allies.

When the Taliban refused to comply, members of Congress overwhelmingly provided the President with permission to carry out military operations in Afghanistan. On the evening of October 7, 2001, in a scene played out on television sets across our nation, United States and British forces began an aerial bombing campaign in Afghanistan that targeted the Taliban and al Qaeda. Throughout this campaign, dubbed "Operation Enduring Freedom," explosions lit up the sky in Kabul (the capital of Afghanistan) and at local airports and military installations. At the same time, statements from the White House assured our nation that only Taliban military and terrorist training camps were being targeted and that food, medicine, and other supplies would be provided to the men, women, and children of Afghanistan.

Not to be upstaged, Osama bin Laden, in a videotape apparently recorded prior to the invasion, condemned the attacks in Afghanistan and predicted that the United States' invasion of Afghanistan would fail, just as Russia's had failed many years earlier. Then, to no one's surprise, he called for a war (or "jihad") waged by all Muslims against the non-Muslim world.

Over time, large numbers of Taliban forces were captured or fled from their mainland positions in Afghanistan and moved to higher ground. Unfortunately, it appears that Osama bin Laden and his close al Qaeda associates went with them. After a bloody battle in a mountainous area of Afghanistan known as Tora Bora, Taliban and al Qaeda forces agreed to surrender their weapons—a move that now is seen only as a smokescreen that provided cover for key al Qaeda leaders, including Osama bin Laden, as they fled to Pakistan, where they still are suspected to be today.

While as yet the U.S. has failed to capture the alleged mastermind of the 9/11 attacks, it has succeeded—with the help of allied intelligence forces from around the world—in capturing hundreds of suspected terrorists. And with these captures we have potentially prevented the planning and carrying out of subsequent terrorist attacks. In addition to capturing suspected terrorists abroad, we also have been able to capture suspected terrorists here in the U.S.

That's the good news. The not-so-good news is that some of the methods and means the U.S. has used to carry out the war on terror have come under scrutiny. A number of new laws, legislation, and enforcement strategies aimed at targeting terrorism have become controversial, particularly those that affect the everyday lives of millions of Americans.

Is this new war on terrorism worth the sacrifice of our precious and hard-earned constitutional freedoms? Will the war on terror unfairly target innocent, law-abiding citizens or residents of the United States—all in the name of rooting out terrorists and protecting our country?

To answer these questions, let's take a look at the central piece of legislation that has prompted them. It's called the USA Patriot Act, and it impacts you, me, and every other American.

THE USA PATRIOT ACT

Acronyms are everywhere. One thing that I learned from my many years in government service is that government cannot—or perhaps will not—function properly without the use of acronyms. No matter what the level of government—city, state, or federal—the alphabet soup of acronyms has become a way of life.

Without even knowing it, we use acronyms frequently in our lives. For example, *SCUBA* stands for *Self-Contained Underwater Breathing Apparatus*. *LASER* stands for *Light Amplified by Stimulation Emission of Radiation*. Likewise, *USA PATRIOT* stands for *Uniting* and *Strengthening America* by *Providing Appropriate Tools Required* to *Intercept* and *Obstruct Terrorism*.

The USA PATRIOT Act (hereafter, the "Patriot Act" or simply "the act") was created after an in-depth review of the legal tools available for law enforcement and intelligence officials to use in bringing terrorists and their supporters to justice. Because of the ongoing threat of terrorist attacks, officials in the Bush administration moved quickly to give investigators and federal attorneys the ability, amongst many other things, to ease restrictions on wiretaps and improve the federal government's ability to share intelligence.

Over the last few years, you probably have heard the phrase "connect the dots" used often in discussions about the war on terror—an obvious reference to the childhood game that we all played in which we followed numbers connected to dots in order to form a picture. This game was simple because all it required was that you know how to count and draw straight lines. If you passed that test, the odds were good that you would end up with a picture: a dog, say, or a bird, or a child playing in a sandbox. And when it was all said and done, you pulled out your Crayola crayons and colored the picture, being ever so careful to stay within the lines.

At the time of its passage, proponents of the Patriot Act argued that the laws in place prior to and at the time of the 9/11 attacks severely limited the ability of law enforcement and intelligence officials to "connect the dots" between investigations being conducted by various state, local, and federal agencies. They claimed they couldn't see the big picture. In effect, the Patriot Act facilitates "dot connecting": it breaks down barriers that prevent intelligence officials from sharing information with other federal law enforcement and national security personnel.

An example of the type of information-sharing "barrier" targeted by the Patriot Act comes from testimony provided by United States

Attorney Patrick Fitzgerald of Illinois, in which he describes his experience with the "wall" between law enforcement and intelligence personnel that existed prior to the act's passage. In recent testimony before the Senate Judiciary Committee, Mr. Fitzgerald stated:

> I was on a prosecution team in New York that began a criminal investigation of Osama bin Laden in early 1996. The team—prosecutors and FBI agents assigned to the criminal case—had access to a number of sources. We could talk to citizens. We could talk to local police officers. We could talk to other U.S. government agencies. . . . And foreign citizens. And we did all those things as often as we could. We could even talk to al Qaeda members—and we did. . . . But there was a group of people we were not permitted to talk to. Who? The FBI agents across the street from us in lower Manhattan assigned to a parallel intelligence investigation of Osama bin Laden and al Qaeda. We could not learn what information they had gathered. That was "the wall."

The Department of Justice (DOJ) cites the Patriot Act as the reason why terrorist activity in upstate New York has been brought to an end. Several residents of the town of Lackawanna, New York, allegedly traveled to Afghanistan in 2001 and were trained at an al Qaeda–affiliated camp. In the summer of 2001, the FBI received an anonymous letter alleging that these individuals might be involved in crimes and were associating with foreign terrorists. Two separate investigations were simultaneously conducted. Without the Patriot Act in place, the law prohibited sharing of information between intelligence officers and law enforcement agents; they could not be in the same room at the same time discussing the findings of their investigations. After the passage of the Patriot Act, however, barriers that previously had separated these investigations were removed, and the result was a quick resolution in the case against the "Lackawanna Six." The investigation ended with the individuals being charged in federal court. All six have since been sentenced to federal prison for terms ranging from seven to ten years.

The Patriot Act contains over three hundred pages of text, and the facilitation of information sharing across agency and jurisdictional lines is just one of the ways in which it aids in the fight against terrorism. Among other things, the act also updates the law to reflect new technologies and threats and imposes tough new penalties on those who commit or support terrorist crimes both at home and abroad—and that's just the beginning.

THE CONTROVERSY
SURROUNDING THE PATRIOT ACT

While many Americans are prepared to give our government all the financial and moral support it needs to pursue terrorists in the wake of the 9/11 attacks, certain provisions of the Patriot Act nonetheless disturb some Americans. For some people, certain parts of the act evoke a time that, in retrospect, seems eerily similar to 9/11: the days and months after the 1941 attack on Pearl Harbor.

After Pearl Harbor, officials were concerned about the possibility that citizens or residents of Japanese descent could be spies providing aid to Japanese forces—in much the same way that officials in the wake of 9/11 were concerned that Arab Americans and Muslims could be supporters of terrorist groups. In response to Pearl Harbor, President Roosevelt made a decision to round up people of Japanese descent and hold them in internment or isolation camps until after World War II was over. The thinking was that by placing potential spies in these camps, the risk of another surprise attack would be greatly reduced. Conditions in the camps were deplorable: Poor waste and sanitation facilities, lack of clean water, and little food were common. Worst of all, many Americans were forced out of their homes and communities simply because they were Japanese.

Because of the sweeping changes brought about by the Patriot Act, some of its critics are concerned that the act was a knee-jerk response to the fear generated by 9/11, and that its use to root out terrorism gives our government too much power—power that can be used to prosecute and deny civil liberties to citizens, especially Arab Americans. Some people fear a denial of civil liberties for minority groups, similar to what Japanese Americans faced during World War II.

Opponents of the Patriot Act also claim that the act invades the privacy of *all* Americans, regardless of their ethnic backgrounds. Under the Patriot Act, the FBI now has the power to access many private medical, travel, library, and student records during the course of terrorism-related investigations—without obtaining a warrant, without observing the standard of probable cause, and without informing the subject or subjects of its investigations. This part of the act, Section 215, essentially permits government officials to require libraries and hospitals to produce their records in the course of terrorism-related investigations. This means that the government may require librarians to turn over details about your reading habits, and hospital personnel to turn over your medical records, all without telling you. Government agents protected by the Patriot Act also may secretly detain noncitizens and use secret search warrants in the course of their investigations.

Opponents believe that Section 215 of the Patriot Act goes too far and is too broad, especially since it allows investigators to access entire databases of records relating to entire groups of people—even if the actual targets of an investigation are just a few specific persons within those groups.

Despite the resistance of many Americans to this section of the Patriot Act, however, use of library records in this manner is not new. In the 1970s and 1980s, during what was then called the "library awareness program," the FBI used its agents to obtain information about potential Soviet spies and supporters. In some cases, the records were sought without a court order—a process that was opposed by the American Library Association—and the program was subsequently discontinued. As a result, many states have taken steps to pass what are known as "patron record confidentiality laws," which protect the confidentiality of library records.

Some libraries in the country have taken novel steps to warn the public about the relevant provisions of the Patriot Act. For example, librarians in Seattle passed out bookmarks warning those who frequented their libraries that their reading choices and document-searching activities could become the subjects of searches by federal agents. Libraries in Santa Monica, California, took this practice a step further by posting signs providing the public with warnings about the new sweeping powers that the Patriot Act afforded to law enforcement officials: "Attention library patrons: The FBI has the right to obtain a court order to access any records we have of your transactions in the library, a right given to them by Section 215 of the USA Patriot Act."

Other parts of the act, such as Section 213, allow the government to search a person's home and then take its time telling them about it—a fact that runs counter to our constitutional expectations about unannounced searches of our persons and our homes. In addition, this portion of the act applies to any subject of an investigation— not just those who are suspected of terrorism.

A leading voice against the Patriot Act has been the American Civil Liberties Union (ACLU), which proclaims itself to be "our nation's guardian of liberty." Through its work in courts, legislatures, and communities around the country, the ACLU and its member chapters aim to defend and preserve the individual rights and liberties of all Americans. As drafts of the Patriot Act were going to press, leaders from the ACLU immediately stepped in and voiced their opposition. In part because of the public awareness campaign the ACLU mounted in response to this issue, two New Jersey towns recently joined the list of 194 communities in thirty-four states that have passed resolutions denouncing the act.

The ACLU's apprehension about the government's new powers under the Patriot Act increased measurably during the 2004 holiday season when news reports out of Las Vegas cited the FBI's use of what are known as "national security letters" to take possession of the travel and hotel records of over three hundred thousand visitors to the city. Under Section 374 of the act, the FBI can gain access to and control of these records—without the permission of a judge or a grand jury subpoena—by drafting a national security letter stating that the information they seek is important to a national security investigation. With respect to the incident in Las Vegas, it appears that the FBI seized records without possessing any actual intelligence pointing to a threatened or potential attack on the city.

The ACLU has also expressed great concern about the provisions of the Patriot Act that allow the "indefinite detention of immigrants and other non-citizens." Section 412 of the act allows detention where the Attorney General has "reasonable grounds to believe" that a detainee is involved in terrorism or an activity that poses a danger to national security. These changes, and some changes that have been made to immigration laws since the events of 9/11, have left opponents of the act concerned about potential abuses that could occur at the hands of the government.

A lightning rod for opponents of the Patriot Act has been the treatment of suspected members of the Taliban or al Qaeda who were captured during the recent invasion of Afghanistan and detained at what is known as "Camp Gitmo," the United States naval base in Cuba's Guantanamo Bay. Human rights organizations such as Amnesty International joined the ACLU in its outcry against the act, particularly as it relates to the treatment of those who could be classified as terrorists or enemy combatants in the war on terror. Amnesty International has cited evidence of prisoner or detainee abuse and torture at Camp Gitmo and emphasizes that many who were held after the invasion of Afghanistan were not brought before a "competent tribunal" to determine their status, as required by the Geneva Convention. It further claims that our government has refused to clarify the legal status of these detainees, ignoring requests from the International Committee of the Red Cross.

IS THE PATRIOT ACT
A GOOD THING OR A BAD THING?

With respect to divided opinions about the Patriot Act, former Deputy Attorney General James Comey of the DOJ has said, "it's become part of the drinking water in this country that there's been an erosion of civil liberties. We have divided into two groups: those who think that's OK and those who don't."

So is the Patriot Act a good thing or a bad thing? The short answer to this question is that the jury is still out. And, most likely, there is no right answer; in other words, the act is both good *and* bad. Every day opponents mount new challenges to provisions of the act and its role in today's world, while, on the other side of the debate, government officials cite successful investigations and prosecutions that would not have taken place if the Patriot Act had not been law. The federal government also reminds us that the act has enabled many successes that cannot be talked about in order to protect national security, the identity of informants, or ongoing criminal or terrorist investigations.

As the debate rages on, most Americans are split over their feelings about the Patriot Act and whether it infringes upon our civil liberties. For example, a *USA TODAY*/CNN/Gallup poll conducted in August of 2003 showed that a majority of Americans believed that the Bush administration "has been about right" when it came to restricting people's civil liberties in order to fight terrorism:

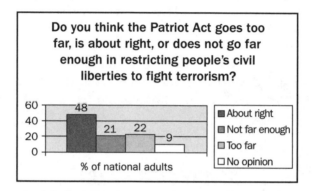

The majority of Americans participating in this poll also indicated that they think the Patriot Act is a good thing for America:

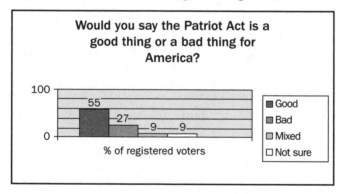

However, opposing views become evident in a poll conducted by the ACLU in December of 2003. In this poll, likely voters in the 2004 presidential election were asked their opinions about the expansion of the Patriot Act and other policies that either give the Attorney General more discretion in the collection of private information or increase federal surveillance and investigative powers. In sum, the results of this poll show that many Americans have strong feelings about the preservation of civil liberties, and that these viewpoints play a very important role in determining how Americans vote.

The ACLU states that the results of its surveys reveal key findings about voters' attitudes toward the government's current direction in the fight against terrorism. In particular:

- The majority of voters have strong reservations about President Bush's push to expand the government's discretion in collecting and scrutinizing private information.
- When presented with a choice, the majority of voters reject the idea of being more concerned about fighting terrorism than protecting civil liberties.
- While voters are largely unfamiliar with the specifics of the Patriot Act itself, they oppose many of its specific provisions and other government actions since 9/11—including the secret detention of noncitizens, the use of secret search warrants, expanded accessing of personal records by government officials, and the requirement that librarians turn over details about Americans' reading habits on request.

No matter what the poll or its result, it is clear that the new powers our government has gained through creation of the Patriot Act have generated intense debate. In February 2005, President Bush asked Congress to reauthorize the act because many of its key elements were to expire at the end of that year. In his view, the act "is vital to our success in tracking terrorists and disrupting their plans."

While there is a lot of information about the act available on government and advocacy sector Web sites, it appears that many of us still remain largely unfamiliar with its actual provisions. No matter what your opinion may be about the Patriot Act and its worthiness in our efforts to prevent or prepare for acts of terrorism, it is important that you become familiar with it. The points that I will reference in this chapter reflect only a small portion of the act and its effect on our ability to combat terrorism. To find out more, visit the Department of Justice's Web site, *www.lifeandliberty.gov*, which provides a summary of the act and updates on its usage. In addition, you can visit the American Civil Liberties Union's Web site at *www.aclu.org* to receive fact sheets about and summaries of the act.

THE FUTURE OF THE PATRIOT ACT

Sixteen provisions of the Patriot Act were due to expire at the end of 2005. Throughout the spring and summer of 2005, debates took place in the Senate and Congress regarding the benefits or liabilities of the renewal or expiration of these provisions. The DOJ and the ACLU have published studies that provide a general overview of government usages of the act—controversial or otherwise—since its creation in October 2001.

In July 2005, the House Intelligence Committee approved changes to the Patriot Act that change the way FBI officials can monitor terror suspects. The committee passed a measure that requires federal agents to provide judges with more detail when they apply for what are known as "roving wiretaps." Prior to the passage of the Patriot Act, federal investigators would receive a court order from a judge that would allow them to monitor *one* particular method of communication such as a suspect's home phone or cell phone. The roving wiretap provision of the Patriot Act allows investigators to intercept phone conversations and E-mail communications on *any* phone or computer that is a subject of a terrorism investigation. The House also overwhelmingly approved the measure that requires the director of the FBI to personally approve any internal requests for bookstore or library records of suspected terrorists.

If this information creates questions or concerns, you should take the steps necessary to get answers or to hold our government officials accountable for addressing areas of concern. The times we live in demand that we not allow new policies or laws to be proposed or continued without our review or comment. To behave otherwise could potentially subject us, our friends, or our loved ones to injustices. And to quote the late Dr. Martin Luther King Jr. in his April 1963 letter from his Birmingham, Alabama, jail cell, "injustice anywhere is a threat to justice everywhere."

Although many of the Patriot Act's provisions may expire, they will not just go away. If you have comments for or against the act after you have read all that you can read about it, you should take your voice to the seat of our government by writing your elected officials. While there are many approaches you can take when drafting your letter, be sure to:

- Explain how the continuance or expiration of the act would affect you or your family, business, or profession, or how it might have an effect on your city, state, or community; and

- Ask your elected officials to provide you with their voting positions when they reply to your letters.

Remember that our country was founded on the idea that we all can play a role in the way government conducts itself. We can do this through our voices or through our votes. As United States citizens, we have the right and the obligation to exercise them both.

THE DEPARTMENT OF HOMELAND SECURITY

The Patriot Act was not the only major legislative change the Bush administration made in the wake of 9/11. On October 8, 2001, President Bush issued an executive order establishing the Office of Homeland Security, the Homeland Security Council, and the position of Assistant to the President for Homeland Security. The mission of the new Office of Homeland Security, with the Assistant to the President for Homeland Security as its leader, was to "develop and coordinate the implementation of a comprehensive national strategy to secure the United States from terrorist threats or attacks."

The creation of this new office sent the message that terrorism would be the administration's top priority and that a comprehensive, unified approach would be taken at the federal level to prevent future attacks. The President's choice for his principal advisor on homeland security matters and the leader of this new office was Thomas Ridge, former governor of the state of Pennsylvania.

The Homeland Security Act of 2002 became law, and its passage set in motion the biggest reorganization of the federal government since the creation of the Department of Defense in 1947. The new law created the cabinet-level position of Secretary of Homeland Security and a new federal agency called the Department of Homeland Security (DHS), which comprises about 170,000 federal workers from twenty-two agencies. The aim of the DHS is to protect our nation from and prepare it for subsequent terrorist attacks, to aid our intelligence-gathering and analysis capabilities, and to enhance efforts to protect our borders, airports, and waterways from terrorists.

To accomplish its mission, the DHS is divided into four divisions: (1) Border and Transportation Security; (2) Emergency Preparedness and Response; (3) Chemical, Biological, Radiological, and Nuclear Countermeasures; and (4) Information Analysis and Infrastructure Protection. It combines the efforts of agencies like the Immigration and Naturalization Service (INS), the U.S. Coast Guard, the U.S. Customs and Border Protection, the newly created Transportation Security Administration (TSA), the Federal Emergency Management Agency (FEMA), and the Secret Service.

What the U.S. Government Is Doing to Stop Terrorism

In addition to creating the Department of Homeland Security, the government has taken many other steps to secure the United States against terrorism. According to information provided on federal government Web sites, these efforts include:

▸ Awarding more than $18 billion to state and local governments to protect the homeland;

▸ Making the countering and investigation of terrorist activity the number one priority of both law enforcement and intelligence agencies. The Bush administration has transformed the FBI into an agency whose primary mission is to prevent terrorist attacks and has increased its budget by 60 percent.

▸ Creation of the Terrorist Threat Integration Center (TTIC) to synthesize information about possible terrorist threats collected within the United States and abroad;

▸ Creation of the Department of Homeland Security Information Network to connect all fifty states and more than fifty major urban areas, and to allow information sharing among thousands of local agencies and the Homeland Security Operations Center;

▸ Doubling the level of first-responder preparedness grants to high-threat urban areas. The Urban Area Security Initiative enhances the ability of large urban areas to prepare for and respond to threats or acts of terrorism.

▸ Signing into law Project BioShield, an unprecedented $5.6 billion effort to develop vaccines and other medical responses to biological, chemical, nuclear, and radiological weapons;

▸ Increasing security and research aimed at protecting the nation's food supply from terrorists, including the addition of millions of dollars in funding and hundreds of food inspectors;

▸ Several initiatives to detect radiological materials being smuggled into our nation, issuance of thousands of portable radiation detectors to border control personnel, and installation of radiation detection portals at ports of entry;

- Improvements made to aviation security: Hardened cockpit doors have been installed on all U.S. commercial aircraft, flight deck crews are being trained to carry guns in the cockpit, thousands of air marshals are being deployed daily, all checked baggage is now screened, and canine teams are now positioned at every major airport to search for explosives.

- Development of a container security initiative to allow U.S. inspectors to screen high-risk shipping containers at major foreign ports before they are loaded in ships bound for America;

- Creation of the September 11th Victim Compensation Fund, which established a streamlined claims process through which victims of the September 11th attacks can receive compensation. The fund will provide a total of about $7 billion in financial aid.

- Development of the public-education campaign "Ready" and its Spanish-language version, "Listo," which educate and empower American citizens to prepare for and respond to potential terrorist attacks and other emergencies. "Ready," the most successful public-service campaign in Ad Council history, delivers its messages through the *www.Ready.gov* and *www.Listo.gov* Web sites, as well as through radio, television, print, and outdoor public-service announcements and brochures and a variety of partnerships with private-sector organizations.

- Training by the Department of Homeland Security of over seven hundred thousand first responders—police officers, firefighters, and emergency medical personnel. DHS also has initiated the National Incident Management System (NIMS) and established the NIMS Integration Center, which ensures that federal, state, and local governments and private-sector organizations all use the same criteria to prepare for, prevent, respond to, and recover from terrorist attacks or other major disasters.

- Creation of the Citizen Corps: In January 2002 the Citizen Corps was launched to give Americans a chance to become actively involved in ways to keep their communities safer, stronger, and better prepared for *all* emergencies. More information about the Citizen Corps can be found at *www.citizen corps.gov*. See also page 66 to learn more about the Citizen Corps and how to join.

THE HOMELAND SECURITY ADVISORY SYSTEM

Once the Patriot Act and the DHS were in place, the question arose: What would happen if our law enforcement and intelligence officials received a tip or picked up "terrorist-related chatter" indicating that an attack was planned or imminent? How would government officials let the American people know—both about the threat of attack, and about what we should do to prepare ourselves and our families for it?

The answer came in the form of a presidential directive, issued in March 2002, that created the Homeland Security Advisory System (HSAS). By assessing threat conditions and employing a unified system of public announcements, the HSAS was designed to inform officials at all levels of government—and the American people at large—about the risks of terrorist attacks.

Imagine that a terrorist threat has emerged. How does the HSAS determine the threat level? As federal officials consider raising or lowering the threat advisory level, they ask four basic questions:

- Is the threat credible?
- Is the threat corroborated?
- Is the threat specific and/or imminent?
- How grave is the threat?

After determining the answers to these questions, the DHS issues advisories in which the relevant threat level is assigned a color:

- Red: severe risk of terrorist attack
- Orange: high risk of terrorist attack
- Yellow: elevated risk of terrorist attack
- Blue: general risk of terrorist attack
- Green: low risk of terrorist attack

As of 2005, federal officials have raised the national threat advisory level from its current level, yellow (indicating significant risk), to orange (indicating high risk) on only four occasions. The orange alerts were issued in response to the invasions of Afghanistan and Iraq and three incidences when terrorist-related chatter significantly increased and contained specific threats.

DOES THE HOMELAND SECURITY ADVISORY SYSTEM *REALLY* WORK?

More than three years after its establishment, the Homeland Security Advisory System has not proven as effective as was initially hoped.

Many Americans admit that they have become "color blind," ignoring press conferences called by federal officials in order to elevate our threat advisory level. Though the United States is fortunate not to have suffered further terrorist attacks as of yet, the DHS has come to be perceived as the "boy who cried wolf": an augur of threats that have not materialized.

A preliminary congressional report issued in 2004 confirmed the existence of such problems with the existing alert system. "The general alert system only numbs the American people to the threats we face," said Moira Whelan, a spokeswoman for Representative Jim Turner of Texas, the top Democrat on the Select Committee for Homeland Security. According to the 2004 report, some federal, state, and local government agencies reported having learned about changes to the threat level only through media reports. The report also stated that the DHS lacks written standards for assessing intelligence and determining whether to change the warning level.

Further complicating the issue is the fact that some cities are always perceived as prime targets for terrorists, and as such, the threat level in these cities is always high. New York City, for example, has remained at threat level orange ever since the September 11th attacks. Moreover, it has been estimated that the cost of lowering and raising the threat level is substantial in many areas of the country; in some cases, state and local governments must spend millions of dollars on security enhancements in response to such changes. To address this problem, many critics believe that instead of putting the entire nation on alert in every instance of heightened threat, the system should be designed to provide warnings or alerts only to those areas of the country that are specific targets. This way, homeland security officials can concentrate their efforts in areas of the country where they are truly needed.

Some credit initial leaders at the DHS with development of the existing Homeland Security Advisory System and believe that former judge Michael Chertoff, the newly appointed Secretary of the DHS, will take steps to improve its effectiveness. In fact, Secretary Chertoff has expressly stated his desire to take a fresh look at the way the Department of Homeland Security shares threat information with the public. In a *USA TODAY* article, Secretary Chertoff stated that he would "mightily resist the temptation to give information out prematurely" and would not want to say that the "sky is falling" if it was not. He hopes to develop a means of applying a risk management approach to sharing threat information, with the knowledge that we cannot possibly be protected against every possible terrorist threat or risk.

In the meantime, the American Red Cross, an agency with a long history of dealing with emergencies, has developed recommendations for individuals, families, neighborhoods, schools, and businesses that could make dealing with the Homeland Security Advisory System a little easier. To access these guides and other useful information about preparing for disasters and acts of terrorism, you can log on to the American Red Cross's Web site at *www.redcross.org.*

The America Prepared Campaign (APC) is another organization that has complemented the efforts of the DHS by providing preparedness information to the public. In addition to being instrumental in designating September as "National Preparedness Month," the APC has partnered with the 9/11 Public Discourse Project—which was created by ten former members of the 9-11 Commission—to build nationwide awareness of the importance of preparedness. Log on to its Web site at *www.americaprepared.org.* (See the "Resources" section of this book for further information about these organizations.)

FURTHER CHANGES THAT MUST BE MADE

While a lot has been done since 9/11 to make our nation safer and better prepared for terrorism, there is still a lot of work to do.

The 9/11 attacks revealed the weaknesses and vulnerabilities of our airline industry. Prior to 9/11, many people had lobbied for steel doors surrounding the cockpits of planes, but for many reasons the steel doors never materialized. Why? Maybe we as a society didn't want to believe that they were really needed? In any case, *after* the terrorists had gained easy access to the pilots, killed them, and then flown the planes into our buildings, it was easy to ask, "why were the pilots so unprotected?" Unfortunately, many experts and government officials fear that our stated enemy is lying in wait to attack us on other similarly vulnerable fronts, such as our rail system and waterways.

The attacks of 9/11 have forced us to focus our resources on specific potential targets, which necessarily leaves others vulnerable. As sixth-century Chinese author Sun Tzu wrote in *The Art of War,* "he who protects everything protects nothing," so we must be careful in our decisions. Choices have to be made, hard choices. What I offer here are my opinions about other changes the government must make to secure our safety and ensure a "new normal," which is surely better than a new terror.

Waterways and Ports

In spite of the efforts of the federal government to secure our nation's ports and waterways, I believe that more can and should be done. For example, we still need to vamp up our efforts to protect our ports and ensure that terrorist-related weapons do not enter the United States. Our ports and shipping routes are part of the backbone of United States commerce, and a dedicated attack upon them would devastate our economy.

It is estimated that of the nearly eight million shipping containers that come through our ports, only about 6 percent are closely inspected. Many terrorism experts and politicians from *both* sides of the aisle agree that this is a problem that can be fixed.

Steven Flynn—an expert on ports, member of the Council on Foreign Relations, and author of *America The Vulnerable: How Our Government Is Failing to Protect Us from Terrorism*—writes, "I'm afraid it's just a question of when, not if, terrorists will exploit maritime containers to do harm in the United States. There's no question the system is open and vulnerable." He suggests three very simple ways to enhance the security of our cargo containers. First, he believes a global system must be in place that allows only legitimate and authorized goods to be loaded into containers. Second, once a container with legitimate goods is moving through the system, there should be measures in place to protect the shipment and prevent it from being intercepted or compromised. Third, each port of call should have a rapid and effective way to inspect containers that cause concern.

Many believe that proper funding is the key to securing our ports. It is estimated that the current level of funding falls about $1 billion short of what is needed. More needs to be done, and I'm sure that more will be done. But in the meanwhile, we need to hold our elected and government officials accountable for removing barriers to further improvement and providing the funding, training, equipment, and personnel needed to do the job right.

Communications

The 9/11 attacks also exposed our vulnerabilities in the area of communication. Communication failures occurred at the World Trade Center. Firefighters inside the towers lacked the equipment needed to maintain contact with their coworkers outside of the buildings, or with their colleagues from the New York City Police Department, both of whom could have provided earlier warnings about the pending collapses. With technology as advanced as it is in our country, the fact that our firefighters lack the ability to communicate properly in the midst of life-threatening events is inexcusable.

Interoperability is the term used in public safety to refer to the ability of agencies to communicate not only with themselves through the use of radio transmissions, but also with other agencies as they work together in response to a large disaster or emergency. Achieving interoperability has been a huge challenge for public-safety agencies for years because of the various communication hardware—some advanced, some not—that is used across the country. A lot of progress has been made since September 11th, thanks to technological advances that allow public-safety agencies to share radio frequencies. In addition, the Department of Homeland Security has created the SAFECOM program (*www.safecomprogram.gov*) to serve as the "overarching umbrella program within the federal government that oversees all initiatives and projects pertaining to public safety communications and interoperability."

But there is still more to do. Achieving interoperability is important to ensure that the lives of emergency personnel and ordinary citizens are not lost because of communication failures.

A NORMAL FUTURE?

As Yogi Berra said, "it's tough to make predictions, especially about the future." Our new enemy is forcing us to make changes—quick ones—in order to make our nation safer. But like the old game in which a street hustler hides a ball under one of three walnut shells, quickly moving them around and asking us to bet on the location of the ball, we too are playing a strategic game—albeit a horrible and dangerous one—with our enemies. Where will the next attack be? How can we muster the resources and attention needed to prevent it? Are our enemies focusing our attention on one area so they can take unnoticed actions in other areas? What are our enemies doing with their "other hands"?

Some critics argue that the steps our government has taken since the September 11th attacks have not gone far enough. On the other side of the debate are those who say that the steps taken have been sufficient; in support of this argument, they point out that another attack has not occurred since 9/11. Based on the evidence, this assumption is a tough one to challenge.

We may never know if the dearth of attacks since 9/11 is due to the billions of dollars that have been spent to protect our homeland, or the increased level of vigilance on the part of law enforcement officials and ordinary citizens like you and me. But no matter how much money is spent to protect our interests, we should never be lulled into a false sense of security or believe that we have achieved an optimal level of preparedness.

We know that al Qaeda is a patient adversary, and that it will not change its desire to attack our country or interests at any time in the near future. But we can take comfort in knowing that with united focus and determination, we, as individuals and as a nation, can make our future safer.

CHAPTER 4

A FAMILY PREPAREDNESS PLAN

Contact Lists, Emergency Kits, and More

Nothing is worth doing unless
the consequences may be serious.
—*George Bernard Shaw*

IN HIS TESTIMONY before the Senate Intelligence Committee in February 2005, director of the Central Intelligence Agency (CIA) Porter Gross expressed little doubt that an attack may happen again on American soil: "It may be only a matter of time before al Qaeda or other groups attempt to use chemical, biological, radiological, or nuclear weapons. We must focus on that."

This statement and many others made on television and radio by a host of experts have had a significant effect on the national anxiety level. According to a 2004 poll commissioned by the National Center for Disaster Preparedness (NCDP) at Columbia University's Mailman School of Public Health, the Children's Health Fund (CHF), and the Marist Institute for Public Opinion, three out of every four Americans believe there will be another terrorist attack on American soil, and their level of confidence in the government's ability to protect local areas has dropped from 62 percent to 53 percent since 2003. Worse, only 39 percent of Americans are confident in the health care system's readiness to respond to a biological, chemical, or nuclear attack.

As I discussed in Chapter 2, without hard data it is impossible to accurately measure the risk of another terrorist attack occurring in the U.S. We and our government officials can only assume that there's a possibility of such an attack—and hope that the possibility will never become a reality. The threat alone, however, should provide enough motivation for all Americans to learn the basics of safety and preparedness, and to have in place emergency plans for use in the event of an attack.

This chapter will provide you and your family with a basic plan to better prepare you for disasters or emergencies that occur in or around your home. Use the checklists provided in this chapter to make sure that you have all of what you need for yourself and your family.

ALL-HAZARDS PREPAREDNESS

When I lecture on preparedness to school officials, I recommend that they not focus their preparedness efforts on acts of terrorism. Instead, they must adopt an "all-hazards" approach, which means they must be prepared not just for terrorism but for anything that may happen: natural disasters, nuclear plant explosions—accidents of all kinds. The fact is that we still cannot predict what a terrorist might do next. We know what prior attacks have looked like, but it is clear that terrorists can be imaginative and cunning. An all-hazards approach will make you better able to deal with any and all accidents and disasters—man-made or natural—that may occur around you.

There's a benefit to this approach: At some point in life, you will probably face an emergency situation. Hopefully it won't be a terrorist situation, but it may nonetheless require you to act quickly. Your preparedness will perhaps save a life or prevent an injury from occurring, or at the very least will reduce your level of stress and frustration.

Let me put it another way. Most of us prepare for a potential flat tire by carrying a spare tire in our car at all times, just in case we get a flat. It doesn't matter if the flat is caused by a piece of glass in the road, by a pothole, or by a spike strip that was placed in the road by members of al Qaeda. As responsible drivers, we are prepared nonetheless. Not to have a spare tire in your trunk is foolish—and so is not having a preparedness plan for all emergencies.

An all-hazards approach to the threat of terrorism is what allowed New York City school officials to handle the situation so well on 9/11. These officials did not have a specific protocol in place for acts of terrorism; rather, the students and staff were successfully evacuated because they followed the rules for fire drills! The conditions created by 9/11 were very similar to those that would have been created by an earthquake. By way of illustration, let's compare the effects of the former with those typically resulting from the latter:

September 11th Attacks	Earthquake
Cause: terrorists (i.e., man-made)	Cause: natural forces
buildings collapse	buildings collapse
loss of power	loss of power
fires	fires
loss of telephone service	loss of telephone service
disruption of transportation	disruption of transportation
loss of life	loss of life

As this comparison illustrates, the consequences of terrorism can be very similar to those resulting from a natural disaster. As a result, protecting yourself and your family against acts of terror is in many ways no different than preparing for any other emergency.

On its Web site *www.ready.gov,* the Department of Homeland Security (DHS) provides valuable information for individuals, families, and communities as they take steps to prepare for disasters and emergencies. The DHS has broken down the preparedness process into three simple and easy-to-remember steps:

- get a kit;
- make a plan; and
- be informed.

For the sake of simplicity, in this chapter I'll address these steps in reverse order: first we'll address being informed, then we'll move on to making a plan, and finally we'll discuss getting a kit.

BE INFORMED

"Being informed" means developing a sense of awareness about your surroundings. When you are familiar with your surroundings, you can tell when something is wrong and have a better sense of what to do if an emergency occurs. Having the ability to tell that something is not right around you is a good thing. It worked for Spider-Man: Whenever he had that special sense that something was amiss, he would say that his "spidey senses were tingling." When it comes to being informed, we all need "spidey senses."

Think about the neighborhood in which you live, the route you take to work, where you routinely shop, hang out, worship, and so on. Make sure you have a handle on how you would handle emergencies in each of these places. Does your place of worship have fire extinguishers? How about that fitness center you go to after work: Does it have fire extinguishers? Do you know where the fire exits are? Does it have everything it needs in case of an emergency? How about those hairdresser and manicurist shops? (Knowing the answers to these questions is especially important with respect to hair salons and other places like them, because a host of flammable chemicals may be present there on a daily basis.)

Be aware of any hazards associated with the location of your home. This means being aware of the likelihood of natural disasters such as hurricanes, tornadoes, or earthquakes, and of physical hazards within blocks of your home that could present major problems for you, your family, or your neighbors if something were to go wrong.

Man-made Hazards

Be aware of any structures in your neighborhood that could cause a major emergency. For example, are you near railroad crossings? If so, do you know what types of materials are being transported in the railroad cars? This is one potential hazard that many of us don't think much about, even though we might cross railroad tracks every day on our way to work or while taking our children to school. On January 6, 2004, one of the deadliest hazardous-material–related train wrecks in nearly three decades occurred in Graniteville, South Carolina, when a moving train collided with a parked train. The tanker car, which was filled with chlorine gas, was punctured. Because of the toxic and deadly nature of chlorine gas, the crashes forced the immediate evacuation of close to six thousand residents from nearby homes and businesses—but not before nine people were killed (one of whom was in his home) and 250 others injured.

In addition to railroad crossings, which may provide opportunities for the transport of hazardous material, there are a number of other locations that may pose a risk to you or your family if they were to become the site of an accident. A partial list of such locations includes:

- chemical manufacturing and storage locations;
- pesticide manufacturing or distribution facilities;
- facilities for storage of infectious waste;
- military installations or munitions factories;
- radiological power plants or fuel-processing facilities;
- fireworks factories and storage facilities; and
- petrochemical refineries or storage facilities.

No one expects you to know offhand whether facilities like these are present in your neighborhood. The best way to find out if you are living close to one is to speak with officials from your local or state emergency management office, usually located in your town or city hall. Your emergency management office will have on file a list of potentially hazardous locations, and will be able to let you know what dangers you and your family might face, if any, because of your proximity to them.

Living near a dangerous facility does not mean that you should pack your things, load up your car or truck, and head for the hills. It simply means that you should add this fact to the list of things you and your family will discuss during your emergency sessions (more on this later), and that you should develop a plan of action for your family to follow in case of an accident.

Natural Hazards

To find out whether your region is vulnerable to natural disasters such as floods, hurricanes, earthquakes, or tornadoes, again consult with officials from your local or state emergency management office, or go to the Web site of the Federal Emergency Management Agency (FEMA) at *www.fema.gov.* Click on the section labeled "Regions" to view a map of the United States identifying your region of the country with a Roman numeral. Click on your region to view a menu list that includes the category "Disaster History." Once there, you can view a recent history of the disasters that have occurred in your region.

Join a Citizen Volunteer Team

Citizens from all across the country are taking personal responsibility to ensure that their families, homes, and communities are safe from crime, acts of terrorism, and natural disasters. The efforts of these "first responders" have gone a long way toward reducing crime and allowing people to react quickly to neighborhood emergencies. Community involvement in disaster preparedness saves lives and makes the jobs of police officers, firefighters, and emergency medical personnel easier.

These teams of preparedness-minded citizens go by different names, but are most commonly affiliated with the Community Emergency Response Team program (CERT) or Citizens Corps. CERT and Citizens Corps are programs supported by the Department of Homeland Security (DHS). You can learn how to:

- put out fires and recover trapped victims;
- perform primary first aid, triage, and cardiopulmonary resuscitation (CPR);
- conduct emergency response drills with city agencies, and outline the roles that citizen volunteers should take during a disaster; and
- develop a database of volunteers who are prepared to lend a hand when necessary.

Find out more information and details about how to join by visiting the DHS Web site at *www.fema.gov*. Your local Red Cross chapter can also help you and your neighbors organize your efforts to be better prepared for an emergency. You can also contact your local emergency management office to receive brochures and training that will help your community better organize for emergencies.

MAKE A PLAN

Every family must work together to come up with a plan for reacting to emergency situations, whether they are caused by fires, floods, hurricanes, tornadoes, explosions, or terrorist attacks—which, as we have discussed, may have the same consequences as any other type of disaster.

Contact Information

The first step in creating your family emergency plan is to develop a good way to let everyone know that you and your family are OK in the event of an emergency. To facilitate this, prepare a list of important contact phone numbers, which must include at a minimum:

- home numbers;
- work phone numbers;
- cell phone numbers;
- numbers of other family members and neighbors; and
- numbers of at least two out-of-town people who can serve as a central point of contact for you and your family members. There's a good chance that local cell and stationary phone lines will be overwhelmed during a disaster.

Make sure everyone in your family has the contact numbers, either on a sheet of paper that they carry with them at all times or stored in cell phone memory.

Incidentally, having an out-of-town telephone contact helped me a lot during the New York City blackout in 2003. Because electricity was down and I couldn't receive updates through television, it was difficult to get a sense of how extensive the outage was. But phone calls to my mother-in-law in North Carolina and friends on the West Coast let me know that others were OK and that the power outage was not the result of terrorism.

You should establish a number of ways to contact your friends and family. In addition to using cell phones and home phone numbers, arrange to send E-mails or leave messages with a commercial answering service. If the emergency is local, you could take the simple step of leaving a note on your front door or your car confirming that you are safe.

Family Planning Meetings

Hold regular family planning meetings to make sure everyone in your immediate household knows what they are expected to do in response to an emergency in your home or neighborhood. Like the yearly reminders that prompt us to change the batteries in our smoke detectors, set up a date and time to sit down as a family and discuss what to do, for example, in case of a fire in your home or a gas leak in your neighborhood that prevents you from accessing your home.

Make sure to cover the following points in your meeting:

❏ **Decide what your child should do if you're not home.**

Do you have a trusted neighbor? Can the store on the next block serve as a safe haven? This would also be a good time to reassure young children that things will be OK if a disaster strikes. Your children will feel better knowing that you are planning together as a family.

❏ Map out an evacuation plan.

Develop a family escape plan to be used in the event of a required evacuation from your home. Everyone should know how to quickly leave your home in the case of a fire or other emergency. Is it safest to exit through the front door toward fresh air, or is it safer to use the windows? If you live in an apartment complex or high-rise building, where are the closest exits to your apartment door? Have you spoken to management about the evacuation plan for your building?

It is especially important for your family to work out an evacuation plan if you live in an apartment or high-rise building, where it may be difficult to exit the building through a window. As with plans for hotels or your workplace (see Chapter 5), the plans for evacuation from your apartment building, cooperative, or condominium should be posted in common areas of the building such as lobbies and elevators, and the overall plan should be distributed and known to all of your neighbors and tenants. Any stairwells and exits should always be free of obstructions such as garbage, trash dumpsters, and cars—yes, cars! (Some people have been known to park their cars late at night in areas near their apartment buildings where they can create obstructions to fire exits.) Signage for exits should be clearly visible.

While it might not be common practice, it would be wise for you to work with your neighbors, co-op owners, or tenant associations to organize fire and evacuation drills. This will help ensure that everyone "knows the drill" when it comes to the safe and proper way to leave their apartments and the building. When you organize these drills, in addition to notifying your landlord or building manager, you should consult with your local fire department. Almost every fire department has a unit that specializes in fire prevention or protection, and these experts—along with firefighters from your local firehouse—can provide brochures, which are especially useful for children, and can help you conduct drills. Such drills will make the task of preventing and responding to fires or emergencies in your home or building complex much easier. Nothing should stop you and your neighbors from organizing your own preparedness efforts.

The Web site of the Federal Emergency Management Agency (FEMA) provides some excellent tips for families on how to develop family fire escape plans. For specific information on how to work out an evacuation plan for your home or apartment, visit *http://www.usfa.fema.gov/safety/escape/*.

❏ **Determine a family meeting point.**

Identify at least two locations where you can meet your family members during or after an emergency, once everyone has safely evacuated. These locations should be near to your home: the store on the corner, for example, or the big oak tree or lamppost across the street—landmarks that family members of all ages can easily remember and recognize. Becoming familiar with these landmarks is important because it will make accounting for your family much easier after a disaster has passed.

Make sure your child knows that if he or she is at a friend's house or elsewhere at the time of an emergency, he or she should immediately contact you or another person on your emergency contact list.

❏ **Run practice drills.**

To ensure that everyone "knows the drill" when it comes to evacuating your home or sheltering in (see page 71), your family should run practice drills. Because emergencies can occur under all sorts of conditions, conduct these drills at various times of the year, at different times of the day, and in different types of weather. Some families prefer to conduct planned drills, while others prefer to conduct them unannounced.

SOURCE: Department of Homeland Security

❏ **Come up with a plan for "sheltering in."**

Your family should also know the steps it will take if a disaster requires everyone to remain within their homes until the danger has subsided. This process is called "sheltering in."

Your family should know that when sheltering in, your general goal is to close all windows, exterior doors, and vents and to remain inside until advised by public-safety officials to evacuate or that the danger has gone away. In the meantime, plastic sheeting will help block toxic fumes or other airborne elements that might affect your family's health. Purchase sheeting—enough to cover doors, windows, and vents—at any hardware store, along with duct tape for securing the sheeting in place. Keep these materials in an accessible place.

❏ **Post emergency information in a place that is easy to access.**

Post all contact numbers, meeting-place information, and evacuation instructions in an easy-to-find place such as on your refrigerator or on a family notepad that is kept in your kitchen. Everyone in your family should know how to contact public-safety officials in your area and other family members. (Remember to include both those who are close by and those who can serve as out-of-town contacts.)

As a reminder, your family emergency contact list should include the phone numbers of:

- family members and out-of-town contacts (the list we discussed earlier in this chapter);
- police and fire officials (usually contacted by dialing "911," though you should confirm that this is the correct number for your local area);
- the family doctor and nearest hospital;
- the nearest pharmacy (many neighborhoods now have twenty-four-hour drugstores, so include those numbers as well); and
- the National Poison Control Hotline (1-800-222-1222).

MAKE A KIT

After we receive warnings of pending natural events like hurricanes, blizzards, or tornadoes, we tend to flock to supermarkets and hardware stores for supplies that will help us through a potential crisis. But what if you get to the store and you are short on cash? And what if ATMs are not working because of a power outage? What if someone in your family gets hurt and you need to locate his or her medical history or a form of identification? Because each of these scenarios is a real possibility, you need to prepare a kit for use at any time.

Your family emergency kit should be ready for use in the event that you must evacuate your home or go without electricity, heat, or water for extended periods of time. Your kit should consist of an emergency supply of water, food, clothing, and other essential items gathered in one place, such as in a backpack, duffel bag, or large container. These containers or kits should be kept in a location that is dry and easily accessible to all of your family members.

The contents of your supply kit may vary depending on where you live. Check with your local Red Cross chapter or emergency management office to determine what, if any, specific items should be included in your kit because of particular dangers that you and your family might face. Infants, elderly people, and people with disabilities obviously will require special items such as prescription medicine, formula, or specialized equipment, and you should customize your kit accordingly. You should also tailor your kit to the climate in which you live: If you live in a cold-weather part of the country, pack items to keep you and your family warm and free from frostbite or other cold-weather ailments. And in hotter-weather areas—Arizona in July, for example—make sure your kit includes sunblock.

On its Web site *www.ready.gov*, the Department of Homeland Security recommends that your family's emergency kit include the items listed on the following pages.

FAMILY EMERGENCY KIT CHECKLIST

MONEY & DOCUMENTS

❏ **Emergency cash** (small bills like ones, fives, and tens is the way to go) and traveler's checks. You can also maintain an ATM account that will let you access a multi-bank network.

❏ **Important identification information.** Include copies of social security cards, birth certificates, marriage records, and driver's licenses.

❏ **Financial information.** This includes insurance policies for your home, health, and vehicle, and savings and checking account books. You won't use these at the time of an emergency, but you may need them afterward.

❏ **Personal information.** This includes medical information for each family member, as well as any wills or powers of attorney.

GENERAL SUPPLIES

❏ Two pairs of latex or, if you are allergic to latex, other sterile gloves.

❏ Sterile dressings to stop bleeding.

❏ Cleansing agents or soap and antibiotic towelettes to disinfect.

❏ Antibiotic ointment to prevent infection.

❏ Burn ointment to prevent infection.

❏ Adhesive bandages in a variety of sizes.

❏ Eye wash solution to flush the eyes or for use as a general decontaminant.

❏ Thermometer.

❏ Prescription medications such as insulin, heart medicine, and asthma inhalers. Periodically update your family's medications to ensure that they don't expire.

❏ Prescribed medical supplies such as glucose and blood pressure–monitoring equipment and supplies.

❏ Tube of petroleum jelly or other lubricant that can be used to prevent dryness, chafing, or cracking of the skin during extreme weather conditions.

❑ Nonprescription drugs such as aspirin or nonaspirin pain relievers, antidiarrhea medications, antacid for upset stomachs, and laxatives.

❑ Flashlights with extra batteries.

❑ Battery-powered radios with extra batteries.

❑ Dust masks and work gloves.

❑ Plastic garbage bags and ties.

❑ Personal-hygiene items.

❑ Whistle.

❑ Cloth face masks to help filter contaminants in the air.

❑ Towelettes or diaper wipes.

❑ Wrench or pliers to turn off utilities.

❑ Plastic sheeting and duct tape for sheltering in (see above).

FOOD AND WATER

❑ Three-day supply of water (one gallon per person per day, and more if you live in a warm climate).

❑ Three-day supply of ready-to-eat foods such as canned meat, canned fruits and vegetables, and pasteurized milk.

❑ High-energy foods like peanut butter and other nuts, dry cereal, granola, and crackers.

❑ "Stress foods" such as hard candy or cookies.

❑ Manual can opener.

❑ Eating utensils.

CLOTHING

One complete change of warm clothing and shoes per person, including:

❑ A jacket or coat.

❑ Long pants.

- ❏ A long-sleeved shirt.
- ❏ Sturdy shoes.
- ❏ A hat and gloves.
- ❏ A sleeping bag or warm blanket for each person.

OTHER MISCELLANEOUS ITEMS:
- ❏ Emergency reference material such as a first-aid book, or a photocopy of such material.
- ❏ Rain gear
- ❏ Mess kits, paper cups, paper plates, and plastic utensils
- ❏ Paper towels
- ❏ Fire extinguisher
- ❏ Tent
- ❏ Compass
- ❏ Matches in a waterproof container
- ❏ Signal flare
- ❏ Paper and pencil
- ❏ Medicine dropper
- ❏ Feminine supplies
- ❏ Household chlorine bleach. You can use bleach as a disinfectant (diluted nine parts water to one part bleach), or in an emergency you can also use it to purify water. Use sixteen drops of regular household liquid bleach per gallon of water. Do not use scented or color-safe bleach or bleaches with added cleaners.

SPECIAL NEEDS FOR
THE ELDERLY OR DISABLED

If you are elderly or disabled or assist those who are elderly or disabled, bear the following questions in mind as you develop your family preparedness plan:

- Do you require any special medication? How long can you go without it?
- Do you have easy access to your doctors' contact information?
- Are there areas in your community equipped to shelter the elderly or disabled for short or long-term periods?
- What provisions will be made for your care during a disaster?
- If a loved one resides in a nursing home or medical facility, how will you be contacted in the event of a disaster? Does the facility have a disaster plan?

Special emergency supplies for seniors and those with disabilities include:

- List of prescription medications including dosage. Include any allergies.
- Extra eyeglasses and hearing-aid batteries.
- Extra wheelchair batteries or other special equipment.
- A list of the style and serial numbers of medical devices such as pacemakers.
- Copies of medical insurance and Medicare cards.
- List of doctors and emergency contacts.

CHEMICAL, RADIOLOGICAL, NUCLEAR, OR BIOLOGICAL ATTACKS

Part of an all-hazards approach to preparedness is preparing for the possibility of a worst-case scenario such as a chemical, nuclear, or biological attack. Terrorist groups such as al Qaeda have made it known that they desire to possess weapons typically used in such attacks. Mindful of this threat, federal, state, and local government officials have taken a number of steps to prepare medical professionals for the damage that these weapons could cause. In addition to conducting training and drills that simulate the fallout caused by weapons of mass destruction, the Department of Homeland Security has developed a program called Project BioShield that takes a number of steps to enhance our nation's biodefense. Such steps include the development and pre-purchase of air-monitoring technologies— aimed at detecting biological agents in the air near high-threat or high-value targets such as stadiums or transit systems—and the development for biodefense purposes of critically needed vaccines and medications, as soon as experts agree that such medications are safe.

While the risks of a radiological, nuclear, chemical, or biological attack may seem exaggerated to you, it is nonetheless worthwhile to educate yourself about how to recognize these types of attacks. What follows is a modified excerpt from a "quick guide" developed by Dr. Lynn Davis, a senior political scientist with the California-based think tank RAND Corporation, outlining descriptions of and appropriate responses to these types of attacks. (The information contained below has been edited to meet the needs of this book. The entire guide, "Individual Preparedness and Response to Chemical, Radiological, Nuclear and Biological Terrorist Attacks," can be ordered from the RAND Corporation's Web site at *www.rand.org.*).*

Chemical Attack

Chemical attacks entail the dispersal of chemical vapors, aerosols, liquids, or solids that have hazardous effects on people, animals, or plants. Chemical agents can be released by a variety of methods, including by bombs or by spraying from vehicles. They

---

*Source: Individual Preparedness and Response to Chemical, Radiological, Nuclear, and Biological Attacks: A Quick Guide by Lynn E. Davis, Tom LaTourette, David E. Mosher, Lois M. Davis, and David R. Howell. Reprinted with permission from RAND Public Safety and Justice.

affect individuals through inhalation or exposure to eyes and skin. Their impact may be immediate (a few seconds) or delayed (several hours to several days), and some chemical agents are odorless and tasteless.

You will know that you are the victim of a chemical attack if you see many people who are experiencing nausea, blurred vision, and difficulty breathing.

Overarching Goal in a Chemical Attack

Find clean air very quickly.

RESPONSE ACTIONS

1. If an attack occurs outdoors and you are outdoors, take shelter quickly in the closest building, close all windows and doors, and shut off the flow of air. If inside, stay inside. Then, to the extent possible, move upstairs, find an interior room, and seal the room. Remain inside until told it is safe to leave, then ventilate and vacate the shelter immediately.

2. If the attack is indoors, follow chemical attack plans specific to your building. If these are not available, open windows and breathe fresh air. If open windows are not accessible, evacuate by stairs to the street or roof.

3. Once protected from chemical agent exposure, decontaminate by removing clothes and showering.

4. When conditions are safe to move about freely, seek medical treatment.

Radiological Attack

A dirty bomb uses conventional explosives to disperse radioactive material across a wide area, although slower and less-dramatic methods of dispersal are also possible and may escape detection. The area affected by a radiological attack could be fairly small—a few blocks—or could cover hundreds of square kilometers with low-level radiation, depending primarily on the type and amount of radioactive material used.

You will know that an explosion has occurred by the blast damage to buildings, but you may not know immediately whether the explosion involved radioactive contamination.

Overarching Goal in a Radiological Attack

Avoid inhaling dust that could be radioactive.

RESPONSE ACTIONS

1. If an explosion occurs outdoors or you are informed of an outside release of radiation and you are outside, cover nose and mouth and seek indoor shelter. If you are inside an undamaged building, stay there. Close windows and doors and shut down ventilation systems. Exit shelter when told it is safe.

2. If an explosion occurs inside your building or you are informed of a release of radiation, cover nose and mouth and go outside immediately.

3. Decontaminate by removing clothing and showering.

4. Relocate outside the contaminated zone only if instructed to do so by public officials.

Nuclear Attack

A nuclear detonation has several immediate effects: a powerful blast that knocks over buildings, high-energy prompt radiation from the nuclear reaction, a strong flash of light and heat, and an electromagnetic pulse that may interfere with electronic equipment. The distance from which those effects are felt depends on the size of the weapon and how high above the ground the detonation occurs.

You will know when a nuclear attack occurs by the bright flash, loud explosion, widespread destruction, intense heat, strong winds, and visible mushroom cloud that such an attack will cause.

Overarching Goal in a Nuclear Attack

Avoid radioactive fallout: Evacuate the fallout zone quickly or, if not possible, seek best available shelter.

RESPONSE ACTIONS

1. Move out of the path of the radioactive fallout cloud as quickly as possible (less than ten minutes when in immediate blast zone) and then find medical care immediately.

2. If it is not possible to move out of the path of the radioactive fallout cloud, take shelter as far underground as possible, or if underground shelter is not available, seek shelter in the upper floors of a multistory building.

3. Find ways to cover skin, nose, and mouth, if it does not impede either evacuating or taking shelter.

4. Decontaminate as soon as possible once protected from the fallout.

5. If outside the radioactive fallout area, still take shelter to avoid any residual radiation.

Biological Attack

Biological attacks can involve two basic types of biological agents: contagious and noncontagious. Contagious agents spread from person to person and include such agents as smallpox, plague, ebola, and dengue fever. Noncontagious agents do not spread from person to person; the primary threat is posed from the initial release of the agent. Such agents include anthrax and tularemia as well as biological toxins.

Overarching Goal in a Biological Attack

Get medical aid and minimize further exposure to agents.

RESPONSE ACTIONS

If symptomatic, immediately see a medical provider for medical treatment.

If informed by public-health officials that you may have been exposed, follow their guidance.

- For contagious diseases, expect to receive medical evaluation, surveillance, or quarantine. If "in contact" with persons symptomatic with smallpox, obtain vaccination immediately.

- For noncontagious diseases, expect to receive medical evaluation. For anthrax, obtain appropriate antibiotics quickly.

For both, monitor for symptoms. In the case of contagious diseases, minimize contact with others.

Leave the affected area once you are on antibiotics, if advised to do so by public-health officials.

PREPAREDNESS FOR PETS

Most pet owners could not envision a scenario in which they would leave their pets behind in the event of an evacuation. The fact of the matter is that many pets are considered family. If you are a pet owner, you should find out now—before a disaster strikes, not during or after a disaster—whether the indoor location to which you and your family plan to evacuate will accept pets.

Because of liability concerns, many locations hesitate to accept pets unless they are designated as assistance animals such as those that provide aid to the visually impaired.

According to the Humane Society of the United States (*www.hsus.org*), in addition to learning about local shelter policies, pet owners should:

- list contact information, including the names of out-of-state contacts, on their pets' identification tags or licenses;
- prepare separate emergency kits for their pets, which at a minimum should include leashes, collars, extra identification tags, food, water, any health records, and proof of ownership;
- have extra portable carriers on hand; and
- prepare a first-aid kit with information about the veterinarians who care for their pets, and forms authorizing treatment for their pets.

In addition, owners of livestock should:

- post emergency contact numbers on their barns or on the fences of their pastures;
- train livestock to board transportation vehicles;
- have a list on hand of neighbors willing to keep their livestock;
- have a supply of feed at an off-site location that can be accessed if their animals become stranded; and
- keep photos and copies of livestock ownership papers.

You should also know that as a pet owner you may not be alone in your concerns for your pet. In Phoenix, Arizona, for example, veterinarians, disaster volunteers, and animal welfare experts are designing emergency response plans for pets and livestock that may be harmed or displaced during wildfires, flash floods, or bioterrorism attacks. You should find out what emergency care your community can provide for your pets and livestock *before* a disaster strikes.

DURING AN EMERGENCY

Sometimes the best response to an emergency is remaining in your home until you receive directions from emergency responders such as police officers or firefighters. Unless there is an emergency in or around your home that immediately affects you or your family—a fire, gas leak, or explosion, for example—first responders may request that you remain in your home, where there is shelter, food, and water, until the danger outside of your home has passed. This approach might be best, for example, if a toxic chemical has been released in your community and exposure to it by humans or domestic animals could result in death or serious injury. (In this situation, you may need to use plastic sheeting and duct tape to cover your doors, windows, and vents, as discussed earlier in this chapter.) Remaining at home might also be the best approach in the event of a fire outside of your home, particularly if you live in an apartment building.

Prior to taking any action, listen to radio or television announcements or contact emergency officials if you can. In some cases, officials will use emergency notification systems such as loudspeaker trucks or loud audible alarms that will alert or advise you about the proper actions to take. Some communities also use a "Reverse 911" calling system, in which public-safety officials make large numbers of calls to residents to alert them to emergencies and provide them with response instructions. Speak with the emergency management officials in your area or consult their Web sites to get a better idea of the ways in which you will be notified in the event of an emergency in your area.

■

There is no better feeling than the feeling of knowing that your family members are safe and prepared for emergencies that may occur in their homes or their neighborhoods. Take the time to put into action the tips set forth in this chapter. Doing so can save your life and the lives of those you love.

CHAPTER 5

A WORKPLACE AND TRAVEL PREPAREDNESS PLAN

Essentials for Work and Commute

I travel a lot; I hate having
my life disrupted by routine.
—*Caskie Stinnett*

DR. ROBYN GERSHON, my mentor and colleague at the Columbia University Mailman School of Public Health, conducted a study to determine what really happened during the evacuation of the World Trade Center (WTC) on September 11, 2001. Robyn and her research staff interviewed hundreds of people who worked in or around the WTC towers and were fortunate enough to be evacuated safely before their collapse. In her report, Robyn identified workplace barriers—corporate policies as well as physical elements of building design—that might affect employees' abilities to respond quickly to an emergency such as the one that occurred on 9/11.

Robyn's work, which I reference throughout this chapter, is crucial because millions of Americans work in office buildings, and many of those office buildings are several stories high. In fact, many of us spend most of our waking hours either at work or getting to and from work, so there's a good chance you'll be in your office or a car, train, or plane, if an emergency happens.

WORKPLACE EMERGENCY DRILLS

Who takes workplace emergency drills seriously? Most of us don't. The alarms and bells ring, but we ignore them, choosing instead to sit at our desks, answer our phones, or finish typing those last E-mails. We know that emergency drills might save our lives, but the risk of an emergency seems so remote compared with the risk of missing our 5 P.M. deadlines.

But here's something to think about: On 9/11, those who survived the initial impact of the planes, the subsequent fires, or the eventual collapse of the towers did so because they followed plans practiced in evacuation drills, not because they followed the directives of building officials. Under the pressure of the emergency situation, building officials in the WTC towers had instructed many employees to remain in their workplaces, even when the buildings were engulfed in flames. Many survivors recalled that they had essentially ignored these instructions, instead applying the information they had learned in prior evacuation drills and getting out of the buildings as soon as they could.

Of course, not all was perfect. Because of the chaotic nature of the situation on 9/11, the evacuations did not go as smoothly as they could have. Many of the buildings' occupants were trapped in stairwells, which in some cases were not familiar to them because they had never been shown these staircases as potential escape routes. Many others were trapped in elevators, despite having received clear instructions in previous fire drills never to use elevators during an evacuation. (The heat that emanates from a fire can draw an elevator to the source of the fire, potentially trapping its occupants with no means of escape.)

If you don't know the fastest and safest exit from the floor and building where you work, ask your employer or building manager for a copy of your building's evacuation or emergency plan, and become familiar with it. Like school principals, all building managers or owners should ensure that their buildings have emergency plans. At a minimum, such plans should clearly outline the procedures to be followed by security, custodial staff, and building occupants during an emergency such as a fire, explosion, or loss of power. Every employee should have access to these plans.

You should also know your company's indoor and outdoor meeting points in case of an evacuation. These locations will help you and your coworkers account for one another in the event of an emergency, and will provide safe refuge until it is safe for you to return to your office. And just as you would with your child's school, make sure that your employer has updated information on the ways to contact your immediate family members in case of an emergency.

PREPAREDNESS AT THE OFFICE

By interviewing numerous former employees who worked in the World Trade Center, Dr. Robyn Gershon and her researchers determined the most crucial steps employees must take to protect themselves during an evacuation from an office building. In particular:

❑ **When directed to evacuate your work space or building, *do it immediately!***

Make sure when you evacuate that you follow the procedures that have been developed and practiced during drills.

❑ **Do not waste time shutting down your workstation, making last-minute telephone calls, or performing other tasks.**

It is OK to take necessary personal items like your coat, house keys, car keys, or cell phone, but only if they are within your immediate reach.

❑ **Keep an extra pair of comfortable shoes in your office or near your desk.**

When it is time to move quickly, sandals or shoes with high heels can make it tough for you to make it out of your office or down flights of stairs.

❑ **Keep a small flashlight with you just in case your work area or stairwell loses electricity.**

You may also want to keep in your drawer a whistle that will allow you to signal your whereabouts if you are trapped in your office area or building.

❑ **Be aware of your limitations.**

If you have a health condition or disability that might make your evacuation from your office or building a little tough, you should inform your employer now—in writing! This kind of notification is important and should happen before an emergency occurs, not during the emergency and certainly not after it.

❏ **Be your own "first responder."**

In other words, use your best judgment about when it is time to evacuate your workplace or office building. Dr. Gershon discovered that some employees in the World Trade Center chose to remain in their workplaces or offices, while others made the decision to leave. The reason some employees chose to stay? They did not receive direction or permission from their supervisors to evacuate. When your "spidey senses" tell you that it is time to go, do what you must do to protect yourself. Of course, be mindful of your coworkers. And if you do decide to evacuate, make sure that your actions are consistent with the plans that have been developed by your company and office building.

❏ **Map an alternate way home.**

You should know at least two different ways to get home, just in case your normal mode of transportation is unavailable. What if the highway on which you usually drive home is closed because of a serious accident, or is flooded because of a water main break? What if the subway or rail train that you take home is not in service because of a power outage or downed power lines? Do you have another way to get home? Do you have a place to stay just in case? Identify nearby hotels or places where you can rest your head if you are forced to stay near your office. Some offices maintain temporary supplies and areas where their employees can stay during a long-term emergency.

❏ **Always have at least half a tank of gas in your car.**

During a disaster you might be forced to take an alternate route home or may be forced to sit in traffic for hours. The last thing you want is to run out of gas when your goal is to get home as safely and quickly as possible.

❏ **Have a way to contact loved ones to let them know that you are safe.**

See Chapter 4 for more information about how to develop an emergency plan for your family.

Preparedness for Employers and Small-Business Owners

On 9/11, there existed a number of barriers to the safe evacuation of the World Trade Center towers, including a general lack of communication among supervisors and managerial personnel during the evacuation, and confusion regarding their roles and responsibilities. Many employees suffered from a general lack of familiarity with the layouts of their workplaces and/or buildings. In many cases, visitors did not know what to do.

Of the many recommendations to emerge from Dr. Gershon's work, perhaps the most important is the suggestion that workplaces conduct mandatory drills and training on a regular basis—particularly for new employees—to ensure that everyone is familiar with established procedures and the design of the workplace, including the locations of stairwells and egress points. Signs and maps should be posted to help visitors navigate their way to exits.

The Department of Homeland Security (DHS) and the Federal Emergency Management Agency (FEMA) recommend that employers of all sizes take proactive steps to prepare their employees for emergencies in the workplace and to ensure that their businesses are properly prepared to recover from disasters. Further information about these steps and their estimated costs—which are not terribly high—can be found at the DHS Web site for businesses, *http://www.ready.gov/business/index.html*, or at the FEMA Web site, *http://www.fema.gov/library/bizindex.shtm*. Notable recommendations include the following:

▸ If you rent, lease, or share office space, coordinate and practice evacuation and other emergency plans with other businesses in your building or facility.

▸ Conduct regularly scheduled education and training seminars to provide coworkers with information, identify needs, and develop preparedness skills.

▸ Include preparedness training in new-employee orientation programs.

> ► Conduct tabletop exercises with members of your emergency management team. Meet in a conference room setting to discuss individual responsibilities and how each member of the team would react to emergency scenarios.
>
> ► Schedule walk-through drills where the emergency management team and response teams actually perform their designated emergency functions. This activity generally involves more people and is more thorough than a tabletop exercise.
>
> ► Practice evacuating and sheltering. Have all personnel walk the evacuation route to a designated area and test the procedure used to account for all personnel. Practice your shelter-in-place plan.
>
> ► Evaluate and revise processes and procedures based on lessons learned during training and exercises.
>
> ► Keep training records.

PUBLIC TRANSPORTATION

I live in New York City and travel by subway to work every day. Chances are good that someday I will be on a subway train that will get stuck in a tunnel for some reason or another. I am not what some folks might call a chronic worrier; after growing up in New York City and riding a whole lot of subways, I am simply realistic. Just as flat tires happen, so do train breakdowns due to derailments, fires, crashes, and many other emergencies. So just in case I am riding a train when such an emergency happens, I keep a flashlight and water bottle in my briefcase at all times. If I ever have to make my way through a darkened subway tunnel, avoiding the electrified third rail or the large host of other things that might lurk there, my flashlight will save me.

Unlike an emergency that occurs while you're in your own car, an emergency that occurs while you're in a public place requires that you have a heightened awareness of your environment.

Shortly after the terrorist attacks of 9/11, the Transportation Security Administration (TSA) was created to protect the transportation systems in the United States—to keep them safe for public use and for use in commercial transport. Whatever the mode of travel that we choose, officials at the TSA recommend that we be vigilant and assist officials as they take steps to ensure the safety of our travel. Suggestions from the TSA's Web site, *www.tsa.gov,* include the following.

Look out for:

- Unusual behavior and suspicious activity;
- Suspicious or unattended packages, devices, baggage, or suitcases; and
- The location of emergency exits and intercoms in stations and on trains.

Observe people who:

- Look lost or appear to be wandering aimlessly;
- Appear to be conducting surveillance using cameras and/or video;
- Abandon items and then leave the area quickly; or
- Openly possess a weapon or any prohibited or dangerous item.

Be aware of items or devices that:

- Appear hidden or abandoned;
- Are connected to wires, timers, tanks, or bottles;
- Appear to be releasing a mist, gas, vapor, or odor; or
- Appear to be suspicious or dangerous, such as canisters, tanks, metal boxes, bottles, and so forth.

Avoid taking direct action if you observe something or someone suspicious. Instead:

- Contact authorities: local law enforcement, security personnel, a train conductor, or 911;
- Remain calm and answer questions as best you can; and

- Avoid using radios and cellular telephones within fifty feet of materials or devices that may be explosives.

If an emergency occurs during the course of your travel, you should always follow the predetermined steps appropriate to your mode of transport. These steps will vary, but in general each mode of passenger travel has evacuation methods and emergency responses that suit it best in the event of an emergency. Take the time to consult local officials and learn the specifics for each. A brief summary follows.

Buses

Prior to or upon entering a passenger bus, you should familiarize yourself with its emergency exit procedures. These procedures are usually posted in bus stations or in bus company brochures or on Web sites, and often are posted on bus windows, ceiling escape hatches, or bus doors. If an emergency occurs while you are traveling by bus, you should follow the instructions of the bus operator or any other responding public-safety official such as a police officer, firefighter, emergency medical technician, or paramedic. If for any reason you are unable to reach the bus driver, you should quickly take whatever immediate steps will ensure your safety—and, if possible, that of the passengers around you—while at all times keeping in mind the posted emergency exit procedures.

Once you are out of harm's way, contact your local emergency officials—and of course your family—to ensure that they are aware of the emergency and that you are safe.

Trains and Subways

Prior to or upon entering a train, familiarize yourself with its emergency exit procedures. These procedures can be found posted in train and subway stations or in company brochures, and often will be posted on the windows, ceiling escape hatches, or doors of the train, or in the back pocket of the seat in front of you. If an emergency occurs while you are traveling by train, you should follow the instructions of the train operator or any other responding public-safety official such as a police officer, firefighter, emergency medical technician, or paramedic.

Many trains and subways are equipped with emergency intercoms, usually at either end of the train car, which should be used to communicate with the train operator or conductor or as a means to report suspicious activity.

If for any reason you are unable to reach the train conductor or engineer in an emergency, take immediate steps to ensure your safety—and, if possible, that of the passengers around you. Any such steps should be in keeping with the train's posted emergency procedures. If the emergency requires that you evacuate the train or subway without the assistance or direction of emergency officials, be certain to follow the outlined evacuation procedures to ensure that you do not bring harm to yourself or other passengers while you make your way through the affected train car and along the train tracks or through the train tunnel.

Once you are out of harm's way, contact your local emergency officials—and, of course, your family—to ensure that they are aware of the emergency and that you are safe.

Planes

When traveling by air, there are a number of steps you can take to increase your level of comfort and safety. Through an initiative called "Fly Smart," the federal government's Federal Citizens Information Center (*http://www.pueblo.gsa.gov/*) recommends that you take responsibility for your own safety by listening to the safety briefing at the beginning of your flight.

Most air travelers ignore the preflight instructions; they think, "if you've heard one, you've heard them all." This is a big mistake, however, because every aircraft—and the appropriate response to every emergency—is different. To become generally familiar with appropriate emergency procedures while you are flying, you should:

- remove the passenger safety card from the seat pocket in front of you, and follow along as you listen to the safety briefing. Always take a moment to review the card before subsequent takeoffs and landings.
- plan the actions you would need to take in an emergency. As part of this plan, count the number of seat rows between you and at least two of the plane's exits.

In the unlikely event of an emergency, be aware of the following:

- **Evacuation slides.** Jump feet first into the center of slide. Do not sit down to slide. Place your arms across your chest, elbows in, legs and feet together. High-heeled shoes can damage slides.

- **Decompression.** Pull your oxygen mask toward you to start the flow of oxygen. Put on your oxygen mask as quickly as possible, then help children and others with their masks.

- **Flotation devices.** Know where they are and how to use them. Life vests—located under your seat, if available—life rafts, some seat cushions, and evacuation slides can all be used as flotation devices.

- **Evacuating the aircraft.** Follow the instructions of crew members, if possible. Stay calm and proceed quickly to an exit. Leave all your possessions behind.

- **Fire.** If you smell fire or smoke, use a wet paper towel or handkerchief to cover your nose and mouth, and move away from the source of the fire and smoke.

- **Emergency landings.** If the plane makes an emergency landing, once you are outside the aircraft, move away from it—and from fire and smoke—as quickly as possible. If possible, help those requiring assistance. Remain alert for emergency vehicles. Never go back inside a burning aircraft.

- **Clothing.** For ease of movement and protection in the unlikely event of an evacuation, it is suggested that travelers wear clothing made from natural fabrics such as cotton, wool, denim, and leather, which offer the best protection in the event of a fire. (Synthetics may melt when they are heated.) In addition, observe the following guidelines with respect to clothing:
  - Wear clothing that allows freedom of movement. Avoid restrictive clothing.
  - Wear low-heeled shoes or boots. Shoes with laces or straps are recommended. Avoid sandals.
  - Arms and legs should be as fully covered as possible. Long sleeves and pants are recommended.

If you have any questions about the appropriate safety procedures on an airplane, ask the flight attendant. Flight attendants are trained for emergencies and know about the safety procedures of the aircraft on which you are traveling.

HOTELS

No matter what mode of transportation you choose, if you are staying overnight at your destination, and unless you are camping out in the wild or staying with relatives, there is a good chance that you will stay in a hotel, motel, or bed-and-breakfast. As is the case with your home and workplace, fires and other emergencies can and will occur in hotels. No matter what their cause—terrorism-related, man-made, or natural—fires, floods, or toxic fumes are all possibilities. Would you know what to do in the event of an emergency?

As is often the case in the workplace, most of us who stay in hotels fail to take drills or fire alarms seriously. I recently witnessed this firsthand when I stayed in a hotel in Seattle. As I was in my room preparing for a conference, the alarm sounded. It was accompanied by a voice message directing the hotel's occupants to evacuate their rooms and the hotel via the nearest exit because of a fire condition. I wasted no time getting dressed and heading for the hotel lobby. On the way, I heard the sound of fire engines and saw smoke near one of the hotel's rear exits. But as I walked past the exercise room on my way to the lobby, I could see that a woman was still on the treadmill, focused on the number of calories that she was burning instead of the possibility that the hotel might be burning. When I knocked on the window and motioned for her to come out, she reluctantly followed my advice, but asked if the alarm was serious because she was in the middle of her workout.

Don't make the same mistake as that woman. The next time you stay in a hotel:

- Be sure to read the room brochures and watch the television monitors to get important safety information that may be critical during an emergency.
- Always find the exits and fire alarm closest to your room.
- If there is a fire outside of your room, always feel the door with the back of your hand before opening it. If you feel heat, step back, do not open the door, and try to call for help.
- If you are able to leave your room safely during a fire, be sure to take your room key with you if the nearest exit is not accessible.
- If you are forced to stay in your room during a fire, telephone for help, turn off the air-conditioning and heating systems, and open your window slightly at the top for proper ventilation.
- To help prevent smoke from seeping into your room, soak sheets and towels and stuff them under the door until help arrives.
- Remember that smoke always rises to the top. If you are

trapped in your room during a fire, stay close to the floor where the fresh air is. Hold a wet washcloth over your face to keep out the smoke and make breathing easier.

- Never try to run through smoke or flames—your clothes could catch on fire and you might be forced to retreat toward further danger.
- Never use any elevators during a fire. They are powered by electricity and could shut down during a power outage, which often occurs during a fire. Moreover, most elevators are heat sensitive and could be drawn toward the fire, trapping you and others inside the elevator.

■

One last thing: When you're at work or traveling, be sure to leave information about your whereabouts with your family, especially in a situation in which your cell phone might not work.

The simple tips presented in this chapter for workplace and travel preparedness may save you and your family hours of anxiety—if not save your lives—in a life-threatening situation.

CHAPTER 6

A SCHOOL PREPAREDNESS PLAN

Your Child's Safety at School

True terror is to wake up one morning
and discover that your high school class
is running the country.
—*Kurt Vonnegut Jr.*

NEW YORK CITY: SEPTEMBER 11, 2001. Terrorists crashed two hijacked commercial airplanes into the north and south towers of the World Trade Center in downtown Manhattan. School officials in New York City were concerned about the approximately nine thousand students and staff in the eight schools located within blocks of the World Trade Center complex.

Beslan, Russia: September 1, 2004. Terrorists armed with suicide-bomb belts and guns seized control of a primary school. Terrorists maintained control of the school for three consecutive days while holding hostage more than one thousand students, staff, and parents, denying them use of bathrooms and access to food and water. Attempts to negotiate the release of the remaining hostages failed, and during the early morning hours of September 3, 2004, law enforcement officials were forced to storm the school to-prevent the killing of more hostages. At the end of the siege more than three hundred hostages had been killed, 156 of whom were children. Many hostages were executed by the terrorists as they were fleeing the school.

Not surprisingly, both of these terrorist events raised serious concerns among educators and parents of school-age children across the United States and around the world. At the time of the World Trade Center attacks, I was the executive director of the Office of School Safety for the New York City school system. Although the schools located near the World Trade Center (the "Ground Zero schools") were not directly targeted by the terrorists, several schools suffered collateral damage from falling debris after the initial impact of the airplanes and the subsequent collapse of the towers. Because of this damage and the resulting difficulties with cellular phone lines, communication with school principals was severely limited, and in some cases nonexistent. At the central office of the Board of Education, we were unable to gather information on the magnitude of the disaster and its direct effect on the students and staff. It was unimaginably frightening.

Parents of the students in the Ground Zero schools were horrified. Many had just dropped off their children when the disaster occurred. Some parents received the news while they were still in close proximity to their children's schools, and were able to take their children home immediately following the event. Others had already arrived at work and were unable to return for their children— stranded by the suspension of bus and subway service and because access to New York City's bridges and tunnels was restricted to public-safety vehicles. And yet another group of parents never made it to their children's schools at all: They worked in the World Trade Center complex, and never made it home that night.

After the events of 9/11, parents and caretakers across the country began to worry that schoolchildren in the United States were in danger. Some urban families moved to the suburbs to avoid sending their children to schools near potential terrorist targets such as landmarks, skyscrapers, tourist attractions, or government buildings. Worse yet was the fear that children and schools could themselves become direct targets of terrorism.

The tragic events in Beslan, Russia confirmed that terrorists are not above using children and schools as targets. Heart-wrenching photos and video images flashed across television screens around the world, depicting anguished parents and the images of their threatened children. News coverage of the event also featured unforgettable images of young children being rushed from the school campus in the arms of police officials or on stretchers, many of them seriously injured or dead.

In the past forty years there have been more than thirty separate school-related terrorist events in more than twelve countries around the world. Since March 18, 1968—when terrorists in Israel attacked a school bus, killing two children and injuring twenty-eight others—it has been clear that terrorists will use children as symbolic targets to get their messages across. Public and private schools, day care centers, and many universities are considered "soft targets": locations in which large numbers of individuals often gather. Other examples of soft targets include stadiums and sports arenas, places of worship, malls and shopping centers, hotels, and office buildings. Such locations generally go undefended or enjoy minimum levels of security, and as such could be seen as easy to attack.

Fortunately, no credible threats toward school or other soft targets in the United States have emerged, but the possibility remains.

As a director of school safety, I have spent significant time since the 9/11 attacks and the Beslan tragedy attempting to address and allay the concerns and fears of educators and parents. The questions they most often ask are: Are our schools safe? and Is my child's school district doing enough to prepare for acts of terrorism? In this chapter, I will address each of these questions in turn.

ARE U.S. SCHOOLS SAFE?

Since 9/11, the United States Department of Education (DOE) has allocated approximately $90 million to more than two hundred school districts across the country to help them improve their ability to respond to emergencies or crises affecting their schools or students.

In addition to federal funding, however, parental involvement is crucial. Every parent should know the particulars of the safety plan in place at his or her child's school. Unfortunately, most moms, dads, and caregivers don't. A national poll conducted in 2003 by the National Center for Disaster Preparedness at the Columbia

University Mailman School of Public Health, the Children's Health Fund, and the Marist Institute for Public Opinion revealed that only a small number of parents have detailed knowledge of the safety plans in place at their children's schools.

The good news is that, of the estimated fifteen thousand school districts in the United States, approximately 90 percent of them have some version of a school safety or crisis plan. A study conducted in September 2004 by a research team from the America Prepared Campaign reviewed emergency or school safety plans in the twenty largest school districts in the United States (for a full report, see *www.americaprepared.org*). The review focused on three areas:

- **The plan.** Each school and district should have a comprehensive plan that details how the school or district would respond to a terrorist attack or major natural disaster. Your child's school should have necessary supplies on hand, like emergency kits, as recommended by the Department of Homeland Security.

- **Drills.** Each school and/or district should conduct monthly drills in accordance with its safety or emergency plan. Drills should consist of tabletop exercises and fire or evacuation drills.

- **Communication.** Each school and/or district should have a process for communicating with parents to provide them with key components of the applicable safety plans—including the procedure for parent-student reunification in the event of a school evacuation—and should ask parents for their input in developing such plans.

The researchers found that while 90 percent of the schools they examined had some form of safety plan in place, some did not have the suggested amount of emergency supplies on hand, failed to hold drills, or failed to communicate the relevant safety-planning information to parents or get them involved in the process. Most schools have taken recent steps to increase their levels of preparedness for small- or large-scale emergencies or disasters, but as a parent you should be prepared to ask tough questions.

QUESTIONS EVERY PARENT
SHOULD ASK ABOUT SCHOOL SAFETY

For parents to gain access to important safety information about their children's schools, they need to do what my mother never had a problem doing: Ask teachers the right questions, and become engaged in the process of their children's education, safety, and general well-being. Being engaged in the process means volunteering to assist the principal in enforcing safety rules during school arrival and dismissal times. It also means becoming a member of the school safety committee, and periodically meeting with the principal (or his or her designee) to review your child's school safety plan so you will know the school's procedures in the event of emergency. You should know the location to which your child will be evacuated if the need arises. Being engaged also means attending meetings called by school officials to keep you abreast of safety problems or other related developments, and not waiting to become involved until a major incident occurs at your child's school.

I cannot tell you the number of times I've attended meetings called by school principals to provide parents with safety updates—meetings that were sparsely attended by parents. I've also attended meetings called hastily in response to crimes or the discovery of weapons in schools. These meetings typically have parents coming out of the woodwork, filling auditoriums to the rafters. But in terms of parental involvement, this isn't the way things should be. Instead, it is important that parents become involved in prevention—not just response.

Meet with your child's principal to discuss the school's safety plan. In particular, you should ask him or her the following:

❏ **Does the school have fire and evacuation drills?**

Most states have required for years that their schools conduct fire drills on a fairly regular basis. For example, New York state education laws require that all schools conduct at least twelve fire drills during the school year: eight before the end of December, and four before the end of June. Check to see what your state education law requires, and make sure that the schools in your area comply.

❏ Does the school have shelter-in-place drills?

Because of the possibility of danger outside the school that could require students and staff to remain safely inside, it is essential that your child's school conduct shelter-in-place drills, also known as reverse-evacuation drills. Just as their name suggests, these drills familiarize students and staff with the steps they will take when they are asked to remain inside the school building until it is safe to go outside. Most of the time these drills require that students and staff stay clear of windows and ventilation areas, and sometimes require that they move to lower ground such as basements or cellars. Keep in mind that if your child's school is asked to shelter in place in response to an emergency, you probably will not be able to gain access to the school grounds or building because of the danger that is present in the area.

❏ Does the school have lockdown procedures in place?

Education officials need to prepare their staff and students for the possibility of remaining inside their classrooms or school due to the presence of an intruder or a violent act (such as a shooting) occurring outside the building.

To address this prospect, school officials have begun to develop what are often referred to as "lockdown procedures." Such procedures entail the securing of doors and windows to keep dangerous individuals from accessing the school grounds—or, in the event that they have already gained entry, the classrooms. If your child's school has developed lockdown procedures, it is critical that students and staff practice them. Many times, the instruction to assume lockdown mode is preceded by a universally recognized signal or announcement such as "Code Red" or "Code Blue." This lets the occupants of a school know that they should begin to take the designated steps. (Incidentally, lockdown procedures went a long way toward reducing student, staff, and parental anxiety during the widely publicized sniper shootings that occurred in Washington, D.C., in 2002.)

❏ **Where are the school's evacuation locations?**

It is important that you know the locations to which students will be evacuated in the event of an emergency. This will allow you to head straight for these locations to be reunited with your child, instead of wasting your time heading to his or her school. This will be beneficial because:

- your child may not be at the school, and you will go absolutely bananas trying to find out where he or she is;

- the school may be a crime scene, in which case the big boys and girls with badges, guns, and flashlights will do their professional best to keep you away from the school and behind police lines; and

- the school could still be a dangerous area, if whatever caused the evacuation in the first place has not yet been resolved.

The school should be able to identify at least three evacuation locations: two in the immediate area and one a short distance away, just in case the entire area near the school is at risk.

On 9/11, we learned the hard way about the value of having three evacuation locations. Prior to the disaster, schools in New York City were required to identify just two evacuation locations. These locations were usually other schools or churches within walking distance. But on 9/11, all of the Ground Zero schools were at risk, so evacuating to other schools would have meant putting the students and staff in further danger. The principals at these schools made on-the-spot decisions to evacuate north or south of the towers to locations that were miles away from the impending danger. In some cases, children were evacuated by ferry to schools in the borough of Staten Island, more than twenty miles away.

❏ What should I bring with me when picking up my child after an evacuation?

If you are required to pick up your child at an evacuation location, be sure to bring your driver's license or another form of certifiable photo identification. Trust me: During an emergency, parent-student reunification never goes smoothly. It can best be described as organized chaos. To control the school campus and keep track of your children, school officials will check the emergency release forms and cards that they have on file. If you haven't filled out one of these forms or updated the existing emergency contact sheet and release form, you should do so immediately! The last thing that school officials want to do is release a child to an unauthorized person. And please be sure to inform any persons that are authorized to pick up your child about the procedures, so there won't be any problems when they arrive.

❏ Is the school equipped with evacuation kits?

Just as you take steps at home to ensure that your family has an adequate supply of food, water, and other basic supplies in case of an emergency that forces you to remain at home for days at a time (see Chapter 4 for more information), the Department of Homeland Security (DHS) recommends that schools take similar steps. Specifically, the DHS recommends that schools have the following items on hand:

- One gallon of water per person per day, for drinking and sanitation. In total, the school should have at least a three-day supply of water per person;
- Ready-to-eat canned meats, fruits, and vegetables;
- Protein or fruit bars, dry cereal or granola; and
- Flashlights and battery-powered radios.

For some schools, especially those that are miles away from hospitals, fire and police facilities, or places where food, water, and other sustenance is available, following the recommendations of the DHS is essential. On the other hand, such precautions are less critical for schools located in more densely populated areas. Not surprisingly, many of the schools in this latter category are located in urban areas, and often are already equipped to provide breakfast, lunch, and in some cases a substantial after-school pre-dinner meal to a large portion of their student populations.

❏ **What forms of communication does the school use in case of an emergency?**

With the many challenges that schools face today, it is important that they establish ways to effectively communicate with staff inside the building and with public-safety officials outside of the school during an emergency. Schools should not be reliant upon one mode of communication, but instead should use many different ways of communicating, including:

- E-mail, either through the use of desktop or notebook-style computers or portable devices such as Blackberries;
- Telephones, keeping in mind that cell phones or hardwired phones may not work during certain types of emergencies;
- Handheld walkie-talkies that are configured to reach staff inside the building and officials outside of the building;
- Pagers (which only allow one-way communications); and
- Public-address systems. Schools should conduct weekly checks of their systems to make sure they are working properly.

❏ **How would you contact me or a caregiver in the event of an emergency?**

When an emergency happens in or around a school, one of the biggest challenges that school officials face is communicating with parents—both to provide them with information they will need to reunite with their children and to control rumors by providing accurate information about the emergency. If your child's school is small, it may notify you through use of a "phone tree," in which a school secretary or other designee calls two or three "initial parents" to notify them about the emergency, the initial parents each call two or three other parents from a pre-established list, those parents call a few others, and so on until all of the parents have been properly notified.

Many larger schools rely upon automated systems to relay messages, or use local media outlets to communicate with parents. The method used is really not important, as long as some method is used to contact you. Most schools will have some process in place to notify you about typical reasons for closing or relocating school, such as a snowstorm or other weather-related event. Ask if this same process will be used in the event of other types of emergencies, and if there is an alternative plan in place as well.

❏ Does the school have a crisis team?

Schools should have staff trained and at the ready to respond to crisis situations occurring in or around the school. Schools often refer to staff members organized in this manner as "school crisis teams" or "school response teams." Having these types of teams in place goes a long way toward determining how the school will operate during a crisis. Such teams usually consist of a person designated to serve as the chair, as well as a deputy team leader who assumes the role of chair in his or her absence. Other members of the team typically perform such functions as coordinating counseling services; notifying staff of emergencies and updating them after hours when needed; communicating with local public-safety and law enforcement officials during emergencies; coordinating notification of the media; and coordinating communication with parents and authorized caretakers.

In addition to supporting students and staff during an emergency, a crisis team can also provide crucial assistance after a crisis, in what is known as the recovery phase. The team can help determine the mental-health needs of students and staff after an emergency and provide referrals to professionals when needed.

YOUR ROLE AS PARENT OR CAREGIVER

In addition to learning about schools' plans for responding to emergencies, parents can also play a central role in preventing emergencies. In addition to getting involved with the overall safety-planning process, ask school officials if you can volunteer at your child's school. Many parents serve as classroom, library, or security aides to help teachers maintain order throughout the school day. Parents can also help conduct surveys to gauge staff and student views on safety. There are many other ways that parents can stay informed about safety at their children's schools; some good strategies can be found online, at the Web site of the National Parent Teacher Association (*http://www.pta.org*).

As you review the procedures in place at your child's school, keep in mind that the contents of a safety plan will vary from school to school and from state to state. The names of plans may also vary from place to place; for example, some school districts refer to their plans as "crisis plans," while others call them "safe schools plans." Though the names may differ, the guiding principles for school-based emergencies remain the same regardless of location.

Once you find out about the safety plan at your child's school, shape your family emergency plan around it. Some parents try to insist on the opposite—that school plans be developed around their family plans. This approach is just wrong. What if parents give their children instructions that conflict with those of the school—for example, to come straight home in the event of an emergency, even if school officials have told them to remain at school? Multiply that directive by a hundred or perhaps a thousand, and the result will be hundreds, perhaps thousands of children disobeying the directives of school officials during an emergency—at a time when school-wide compliance and cooperation is most needed. Chaos ensues.

Respect your school's safety plan. When your child is in school, he or she should generally remain in school, following the directions of school officials. We should not expect our children to go against the directions and expectations of school officials during a disaster. We should not expect our children to make their way home to participate in our family emergency plans if it means running out on their teachers and their instructions. Trust that school officials will do the right thing.

Special Needs

If you are a parent or caretaker of a limited-mobility student, make sure that the school staff takes your child's needs into account during an emergency. Because students with limited mobility have unique needs during an evacuation, it is important that there be adults designated to account for them, assist them, and ensure their safety. School officials should take the prudent step of letting local public-safety officials know about the number of students with limited mobility so that these officials can keep their needs in mind as they respond to an emergency at the school.

If you are a parent of a child with special needs, you should also:

▸ **Ensure that a written portion of the school safety plan addresses the safe-evacuation needs of all staff and/or students who will require assistance during an emergency or drill.** Because every child with a disability will have unique needs, ensure that there is an individual plan designed to meet those needs. You should help with the development of this plan and provide school officials with extra medications or equipment that might be needed for your child in the event that he or she must be sheltered at a predesignated evacuation site. Your plan should also include a person who is aware of classrooms or areas in the school where disabled students might be found during an emergency, and who has been trained and designated to provide assistance to your child and others during an evacuation. Many schools also designate specific locations to serve as secure, temporary areas of refuge or rescue for disabled students until help arrives. Such locations are usually identified by signage that is clearly visible to emergency personnel from the exterior of the school.

▸ **Ensure that your child participates in all fire, bomb scare, or shelter-in-place drills conducted by the school.** These drills are an opportunity to rehearse the process of evacuating your child and others who might be disabled. If you believe that your child is in need of special accommodation during these drills, discuss his or her needs with school officials and keep your concerns or agreement on file with the school in writing.

ARE OUR SCHOOLS PREPARED FOR THE THREAT OF TERRORISM?

I believe that our nation's schools have come a long way toward meeting the needs of the new era that we live in. Despite this progress, we must recognize that schools are not designed to be fully prepared for large-scale emergencies or disasters. Schools are in the business of educating children and preparing them for gainful employment—not preparing them for disasters. (I doubt that a young aspiring teacher is sitting in college as we speak, plugging away at grueling education courses because he or she wants to evacuate students during a bomb scare.)

Whether they are responding to a school shooting, the death of a student from a weekend car accident, or a large fire that destroys a school, educators are fully prepared for emergencies only when they tap into the resources of their local communities.

That is why it's important for schools to develop what I call "registries of care"—lists of community-based organizations and professionals that will be on call when schools need them during a disaster. Your school is best prepared if it has a registry of care that includes, but is not limited to, the following types of organizations:

- places of worship such as churches, synagogues, and mosques, and other faith-based organizations;

- local YMCAs, YWCAs, and after-school centers;
- local mental-health and family health care clinics;
- local Red Cross offices;
- parent support groups;
- key governmental agencies (including twenty-four-hour, seven-day-a-week contact information); and
- construction firms and equipment suppliers that can perform emergency work or provide emergency supplies.

The persons chosen to provide care for children during and after a disaster must be credentialed, experienced, and sensitive to the needs of the particular student population. And the best time to determine if a provider or volunteer has legitimate credentials is before a disaster strikes—not during the disaster, and certainly not after it.

The bottom line is that school is the safest place for our children while we are at work or away from our homes—a fact that has been confirmed repeatedly by annual studies. While many of these studies tend to focus on the incidence of crime, schools are also the safest place for your child in the event of a neighborhood emergency or disaster.

Because they are staffed with child-friendly professionals, schools can provide needed shelter and care for our children during an emergency until they are properly reunited with their parents or caretakers. Becoming part of the planning process can help parents and community members ensure that school safety plans are tailored to meet the needs of their unique school and community populations. So visit your child's school, knock on the door, and offer your services. Your child and his or her school will be the better for it!

CHAPTER 7

TALKING TO KIDS ABOUT TERRORISM AND VIOLENCE

A Psychological Preparedness Plan

Remember: As far as anyone knows,
we're a nice normal family.
—*Homer Simpson,* The Simpsons

In time, perhaps, we will mark
the memory of September 11th in
stone and metal, something
we can show children as
yet unborn to help them
understand what happened on
this minute and on this day.
—*George W. Bush*

WHEN THE TERRORIST ATTACKS OCCURRED in lower Manhattan on 9/11, the one person I did not feel was in immediate physical danger was my son, Tyler. At the time, Tyler was an eleven-year-old sixth-grader at a middle school in Queens, New York. His school was located about thirty miles from the disaster area, so I knew that he was not in immediate danger and that, most likely, he would be able to get home without a lot of extra trouble.

I was concerned, however, that Tyler would be worried about my wife, Kim, and me. I was sure he knew that we would both be involved with the rescue effort in some way, and I wanted to get him the message that we were safe. I didn't want him to imagine disaster scenarios that were even worse than the reality of the situation. Luckily, the staff at Tyler's school decided to provide only limited information about the attacks to the children and allow the school to function "normally," only releasing children early if their parents or an authorized caretaker came to the school to pick them up. Tyler remained in school until dismissal, boarded his school bus at the regular time, and headed home to the care of his babysitter.

I finally had the chance to speak with Tyler at about midday on September 11th, and I assured him that his mother and I had not been hurt. We spoke briefly about the events of the day, but I treaded carefully, because I honestly did not know what to say. A great parental speech did not come to me; I was in shock, too. But I knew that we would have to talk about it at some point.

For me, the events of 9/11 proved that every family's emergency plan should include provisions for psychological preparedness. But what exactly does this mean?

HOW DO CHILDREN REACT TO DISASTERS?

Parents are supposed to make things right, and give children that much-needed "power hug" when bad things happen. Before 9/11, I had a lot of success dealing with the bogeyman and his gang of associates. I even used my Brooklyn street smarts to engage in a battle or two with ghosts or demons in Tyler's bedroom. I always won! But the demons from 9/11 were new. These demons scared me, too.

I knew that I had to tell Tyler that things were going to be OK: That was the party line, and every parent in the city was telling his or her child the same thing. Regardless of one's ethnic background, religious affiliation, income level, or place of residence, you had to let your son, daughter, grandchild, niece, or nephew know that things were going to be alright. You told your children this, even though as an adult you had difficulty convincing yourself that it was true.

This is what parents and adults do: We present ourselves as towers of strength for our children. We do this despite knowing that in most cases, because of the crazy, complex, and sometimes violent world we live in, we cannot always provide our children with the safety and security they deserve and expect.

One unseasonably warm evening in October after things had started to settle down a bit—and after I had taken care of the needs of *every other child in the city* (something I would do again in a heartbeat)—I sat down with my son to get a sense of how he was handling things. Our home in Brooklyn lies in the landing path of planes destined for New York's LaGuardia Airport, and from our front steps you can watch the planes as they make their final approaches. We sat on our front steps and watched planes come in, and this presented the perfect opportunity for me to begin a conversation with Tyler about the terrible attacks.

We had flown together to Disney World the previous summer, and I knew Tyler had not then been afraid to fly. I began our conversation by asking him if he wanted to take another trip to Florida for a warm vacation. His immediate answer was "no," and he explained that this was because he did not like the turbulence of flying. I knew right away that this was a convenient answer, a way of masking his true feelings; in reality, he did not want to fly again because of the terrorist attacks. Tyler then asked me to explain why the hijackers had done what they did, and why they had killed so many innocent people. He asked if we would ever be able to ride our bikes near the World Trade Center again, as we had done so often before. (The original path was destroyed, but thankfully was rebuilt so that cyclists can once again ride their bikes down to lower Manhattan.) Maybe he was wondering what would come next. He had felt safe near the World Trade Center, and now it was gone. What other place might disappear?

We may never know all the ways in which the elementary-school children in lower Manhattan were affected by 9/11. Just as these children were lining up for their fourth day of school, they heard a mighty roar in the normally quiet Manhattan sky and looked up to see the first hijacked plane flying low through the skyline. Then they saw it crash into the World Trade Center. One of those children looked up at the flaming towers, saw people jumping out of the windows, and in the way that only a child can, exclaimed, "Look, the birds are on fire."

We may never fully understand how the classmates of the children who died in the plane that crashed into the Pentagon will be affected in the long term. Maybe they feel guilty that they weren't on the plane. Maybe they will wonder for years to come, "Why was it them and not me?"

Most of all, we may never know the effects of 9/11 on the thousands of children who watched the horrific events unfold live on TV—both in their classrooms and countless times in the days and weeks after the disaster. Indeed, television played an important role in the way that children processed these attacks. Thanks to live feeds from major television networks, classrooms around the country provided children and teachers on 9/11 with on-the-spot information and updates about the disaster. Before children returned home that evening, many had already seen graphic coverage of the attacks. Footage of the planes approaching their targets was shown over and over again on cable and network TV, and children who were at home unsupervised witnessed these dramatic events over and over again as they huddled around their television sets.

Dr. Christina Hoven, a colleague of mine from the Columbia University School of Public Health, led a landmark study on how the attacks of 9/11 affected children's well-being. Her study revealed that almost two-thirds of New York City public-school children spent most of their time after the disaster learning about the terrorist attacks from TV.

Many journalists were initially unaware of the effects that repeat coverage of the 9/11 attacks would have on families, and on younger children in particular. News organizations usually take responsible steps to edit and tone down the delivery of controversial news stories. In the case of the 9/11 attacks, however, new rules came into play. For example, because many people in the targeted cities were stranded in the streets or in transportation venues, the extent of the attacks could not fully be communicated to them—and, as a result, the details of the disaster were not fully known to many people. This meant that repeated coverage of the attacks was in some respects necessary to fully inform the public. Adding to the complexity of the situation was the fact that events relating to the disaster continued to unfold throughout the day and night.

One important lesson learned from studies conducted after the 9/11 attacks is that watching events like these on television or reading about them in newspapers can be overwhelming, and can make younger children feel vulnerable and unsafe. For example, research conducted in the spring of 2003 by the Henry J. Kaiser Family Foundation revealed that, because young children are unable to distinguish between live pictures and replays, many believed that the catastrophe that they saw replayed on television was in fact *happening over and over again.* When they watched footage of 9/11 on television without supervision or proper explanation, their levels of stress and anxiety increased.

After the domestic terrorist bombing in 1995 of the Murrah Federal Building in Oklahoma City, researchers found that some middle-school children who lived over one hundred miles away from Oklahoma City displayed symptoms of distress—so much so that their performances in school and at home were affected for as long as two years after the bombing. Those children who attended middle school near the blast site were greatly affected by repeated images on television of young children being rushed from the disaster site. This coverage lasted for several days and weeks after the event, and resumed in force when the criminal proceedings began many months later.

An article from the November 2001 *New England Journal of Medicine* detailed a national study, conducted days after 9/11, of parents with children between the ages of five and eighteen. Among other things, this study revealed that:

- On average, children watched three hours of television news on 9/11. Younger children watched about an hour or less, and older children (mostly teenagers) watched five hours or more; and

- One-third of parents admitted to limiting their children's exposure to coverage of the terrorist attacks. Parents who did not limit their children's exposure reported that their children experienced more stress symptoms the more TV they watched.

So the question for parents is, how do we ensure that the traumatic events our children learn about on TV will not have a long-term effect on their lives? To answer this question, let's take a look at a few tips from the experts.

HELPING KIDS COPE WITH VIOLENCE AND TERRORISM

How much information about terrorism is too much for children? How much is too little? What sort of information is age-appropriate? Should we assure our children that things will be alright? Or should we tell them the truth: that we live in a different world now, a world where there are no guarantees that this will be the last terrorist attack they will see in their lifetimes? Because of the magnitude of the 9/11 disaster and the possibility of subsequent terrorist attacks, it is important that parents, caretakers, babysitters, nannies, au pairs, teachers, day care providers—in short, anyone who cares for children—be equipped with the best strategies for helping children cope with terrorism.

Television

Given the damaging effects of repeated exposure to disaster footage, it is increasingly important that you monitor your children's access to the media—especially television and the Internet—to make sure the messages they receive are accurate, timely, and not too intense.

In 1998, the National Television Violence Study revealed that:

- Nearly two out of three TV programs contain some violence—an average of about six violent acts per hour;
- Children who watch a lot of TV news tend to overestimate the prevalence of crime and may perceive the world to be a more dangerous place than it actually is.

Based on three years of research, the National Television Violence Study examined the frequency and levels of violence in many different types of television shows, including documentaries, dramas, talk shows, police shows, comedies, cartoons, and children's shows. The research team also examined the effects of this violence on children. Among other things, the study confirmed that:

- Younger viewers are more likely to perceive fantasy and cartoon violence as realistic, making this type of content more problematic for children of young ages;
- Younger children have difficulty "linking" scenes together—that is, making intellectual sense of events occurring at different points in a program. Therefore, if punishment for violence is separated temporally from the violence itself, that punishment—and any deterrence it might otherwise create—may go unnoticed by a young child;
- On account of the two factors listed above, children below the age of seven may be especially vulnerable to the effects of TV violence.
- There is substantial evidence that viewing violence on television creates potentially harmful effects for children. In particular, repeated viewing of violent television shows promotes aggressive attitudes and behaviors.

In addition to violence on television, our children can also be subjected to violence in video games that they purchase, rent, play on their computers, or download from the Internet. To help limit the amount of violence to which our children are exposed—though eliminating such exposure is next to impossible—parents should keep in mind the following tips:

❏ **Limit the amount and frequency of television watching.**
When I was growing up in the sixties, we had only one television in our house. Having one television meant that my sisters and I had to learn the real meaning of the word "share" early in our lives. It also meant that there was a limit to the amount of time we could spend staring at "the boob tube." Limit the amount of time that your child is allowed to watch television, and do not let the TV become the "great American babysitter." Younger children should see a link between doing their homework, doing their chores, and

watching television; if they complete the former, they can be rewarded with the latter. It worked for Mama Thomas, and it can work for you!

❏ **Use the television–ratings system and other forms of parental guidance to help you make choices.**

In conducting the National Television Violence Study, researchers examined the violence ratings that are applied to television shows, and the ways in which parents use these ratings to make television-viewing choices for their children. The ratings comprise six distinct categories, and are briefly displayed in the upper-left corner of the TV screen at the beginning of each new show (except for sports and news shows). They were introduced by the Clinton administration in 1997, and were designed to provide viewers with information that could help them make better choices for themselves and their families. To find out more about these ratings and how they work, you can visit the TV Parental Guidelines Web site at *http://www.tvguidelines.org/default.asp.*

While it is not a perfect system, the ratings system can be used along with previews from television guides or newspapers to help you decide what shows your children are allowed to watch. (See the box below, "Understanding TV Ratings," for more on the ratings system.) As your kids get older, they will need to develop a sense of independence, and you'll ultimately need to trust them more and more. But we can never let them think we won't be there to protect them from things that could harm their development.

Understanding TV Ratings

The icons that appear in the upper-left corner of your TV screen are designed to help you decide what's suitable for your children to watch. In decreasing order of suitability for kids, here's what they mean:

ALL CHILDREN
This program is designed to be appropriate for all children. Whether animated or live-action, the themes and elements in this program are specifically designed for a very young audience, including children from ages two to six. This program is not expected to frighten younger children.

DIRECTED TO OLDER CHILDREN
This program is designed for children age seven and above. It may be more appropriate for children who have acquired the developmental skills needed to distinguish between make-believe and reality. Themes and elements in this program may include mild fantasy violence or comedic violence, or may frighten children under the age of seven. Therefore, parents may wish to consider the suitability of this program for their very-young children.

DIRECTED TO OLDER CHILDREN— FANTASY VIOLENCE
For those programs where fantasy violence may be more intense or more combative than other programs in this category, such programs will be designated TV-Y7-FV.

GENERAL AUDIENCE
Most parents would find this program suitable for all ages. Although this rating does not signify a program designed specifically for children, most parents may let younger children watch this program unattended. It contains little or no violence, no strong language, and little or no sexual dialogue or situations.

TV PG
PARENTAL GUIDANCE SUGGESTED
This program contains material that parents may find unsuitable for younger children. Many parents may want to watch it with their younger children. The theme itself may call for parental guidance and/or the program contains one or more of the following: moderate violence (V), some sexual situations (S), infrequent coarse language (L), or some suggestive dialogue (D).

TV 14
PARENTS STRONGLY CAUTIONED
This program contains some material that many parents would find unsuitable for children under fourteen years of age. Parents are strongly urged to exercise greater care in monitoring this program and are cautioned against letting children under the age of fourteen watch unattended. This program contains one or more of the following: intense violence (V), intense sexual situations (S), strong coarse language (L), or intensely suggestive dialogue (D).

TV MA
MATURE AUDIENCE ONLY
This program is specifically designed to be viewed by adults and therefore may be unsuitable for children under seventeen. This program contains one or more of the following: graphic violence (V), explicit sexual activity (S), or crude indecent language (L).

SOURCE: TV Parental Guidelines (*www.tvguidelines.org*)

❏ **Use the parental controls on your television or cable/satellite box.**

With the busy lives we all lead, we can't be with our children every time they watch television. But behold, technology has come along to save the day! Engage the parental controls on your television set or cable/satellite box: Lock out certain channels during times of the day when you or another adult cannot supervise your child's channel selection, or at times—such as late at night—when television shows featuring violence or other adult material are more likely to be shown.

❏ **If you see something you don't like, make some noise!**

I agree with the folks who conducted the National Television Violence Study. They suggest that you tell the owners of your local television cable and satellite companies about programming you think is too violent and should not be marketed to children. They also suggest that you contact the Federal Communications Commission (FCC) or your local elected officials about your concerns. Using your voice will go a long way toward bringing about change—after all, it worked for us in New York City after the 9/11 attacks. Because of the effect that news footage of the attacks was having on our children, we were able to persuade the television networks to cut back on the number of times they replayed it. Use your voice: It *can* make a difference.

Communication

What are the best ways to communicate with our kids about terrorism and violence? According to the experts, parents should keep the following tips in mind:

❏ **Take a few minutes every day to talk to your child.**

Because of our hectic lives, it can be more difficult than ever for families to gather together and discuss the events of the day. But whether it's during a walk or while sitting in traffic, it is important that you find time to talk with your children about this new era in which we live.

In addition to providing an opportunity for you to talk with your kids about current events—including your child's feelings about war and acts of terrorism—these moments will also provide quality time to talk about school, love, clothes, and whatever else is on your child's mind. Of all of the family values that have waned over the years, that of having a good old-fashioned talk with your kids is perhaps the one that matters most.

❏ **Encourage your child to ask questions about terrorism and world events.**

Every parent or caregiver should find time to talk more with his or her children regarding their fears about terrorism and violence—or anything else that troubles them. Do not assume that you know what your children are thinking and feeling; the recent increase in news about terrorism and violence around the world might affect them in ways you never imagined. Our children take what they see or hear, put it all into that human blender known as their brains, press the "puree" button, and mix it all up with rumor, gossip, and fear. Who knows what comes out in the end?

When speaking with your child, don't gloss over acts of terrorism or other potentially frightening events, because doing so could make these events seem more threatening. Think back to those times when our parents chose not to talk about events that occurred in our neighborhoods or that we saw on television. Experts say that this type of behavior or silence in response to our children's curiosity suggests that what has occurred is simply too horrible to speak about—a suggestion that could cause our children to become even more curious and anxious.

As part of your ongoing conversation, reassure your children that no matter what has happened, you (and the government) are taking all possible steps to keep them safe. The times we live in require more than ever that we restore the confidence of our families and children in the safety of our homes, communities, and schools.

The Tough Questions Kids Ask

When speaking with our children during times of crisis, we should encourage them to ask questions, and we should answer their questions in a direct manner so they can better understand the answers and develop ways to cope. Parents often get asked tough questions—ones for which we don't even know the answers. But we need to do our best. Your kids will often turn to you for guidance, and how you answer the "big questions" will undoubtedly have a great impact on your child's understanding of the world and of his or her place in it. Keep in mind, however, that your answers to these questions will vary, depending on your child's age.

The following is a set of answers to some of the tough questions kids tend to ask. Inevitably, your answers will be different—based on your own unique political, religious, and cultural views. But perhaps these samples can provide a useful starting point:

▸ **Why are we at war?** People sometimes disagree with each other because they want different things. When this happens, the very best thing to do is sit down and talk about it. Remember last week when you and Mary couldn't agree on whether you wanted to swim in the pool or jump on the trampoline? Well, what did you do? Remember . . . you talked about it and decided to jump for a while and then swim. This solution made you both happy. That was a great thing you and Mary did. I was very proud of you! War happens when leaders of different countries want different things, and they sit down and talk and still can't figure out what to do. War is not a good thing. But sometimes it happens.

▸ **Why are people being killed?** That is the very worst part of war. It makes me sad to think of people getting killed. But there are times when it is the right thing. Remember when we talked about the war with Germany? The German soldiers were doing such terrible things that they had to be stopped, even if that meant killing them.

▸ **Are some people evil?** Some people do really bad things to other people. We don't always know why they do it. Maybe someone did something bad to them and they are angry. But whatever the reason, it is not OK to hurt someone unless you have to hurt them in order to protect yourself.

▸ **Is our country better than theirs?** We are not perfect, but there sure are a lot of great things about our country! We have the freedom to do many things, and that is something that is very important to me. But remember: There are some pretty great things about other countries, too. So, no country is necessarily "bad." What is bad is when the leaders or people of a country kill other people or deny them their freedoms. But that doesn't make the whole country bad. The individuals who live in other countries aren't bad. They have families—mothers, fathers, kids, grandparents, and aunts and uncles—just like us. Let's look on the world map and see if we can find [the country you're discussing], then read a little about the people who live there.

▸ **Are all Muslims terrorists?** No, not at all. The group of people who attacked our country on 9/11 was a small group. Most Muslims don't think or act that way. It is important not to assume things about a person just because of his or her religion or background. One of the greatest things about our country is how many different kinds of people live here. Think about your class at school: Marianne's family came from Korea, Robert's family from Cuba, and Tony's family from Italy! It's fun to be friends with people from all over the world.

■

As I mentioned earlier, these answers are just guides; your own answers will, of course, reflect your own personal worldview. You don't have to make things up; if your child asks a question with which you also struggle, it's OK to tell your child "I'm confused by this, too." The most important thing is to engage him or her in conversation when he or she asks questions, and to be comfortable with the answers that you give.

❏ **Don't "define deviancy down."**

In the early 1990s, Daniel Patrick Moynihan, the late United States senator from New York, wrote an essay in which he coined the phrase "defining deviancy down." He used this term to refer to what happens when a society or its leaders begin to view certain deviant acts as normal, and therefore acceptable. In his essay, Senator Moynihan recalled reading an article in the *New York Times* about seven people being found murdered in the Bronx. In his view, the article had focused more on a young child who had been found alive than it had on the seven people who were murdered. It seemed to him that the act of mass murder was essentially being overlooked—and thus, in some ways, accepted. In his mind, this type of behavior had somehow become "normal" in our society.

In the days after 9/11, I thought often of Moynihan's phrase, "defining deviancy down." When you speak with your child about terrorism or war, it is critical that you do not position war and violence as somehow "normal" or "acceptable." While we know that our world has changed dramatically since 9/11, it is important that our children see hope and promise—that they believe there will be peace and an end to the conflicts we now face. We should reassure our children, and encourage them to be the best example of what is right with our country and tolerant of the views of others. We should explain that the violent events of 9/11 were by no means normal, and that violence is not an acceptable means of expressing dislike for a person or viewpoint. We should tell them that terrorism is not something we must simply accept. Changing the views of the terrorists who mean us harm will take time, but in time it can be done.

❏ **Watch for signs that your children might be distressed by the violence or threats of terrorism to which they are exposed.**

When we address the needs of children after a disaster or traumatic event like 9/11, we should "define resiliency down." By this I mean that we should "lower" the definition of resiliency: Use *children's measures* of what is good for children rather than *adults' measures.* It means we should err on the side of caution and assume that children will be sensitive about violent events they witness in real life or on TV.

As parents, we need to observe the reactions of our children to traumatic events. This is not a simple thing to do. Some children may not display signs of distress right away, and some may not display such signs at all. In fact, experts from the National Center for Children Exposed to Violence at the Yale University Child Study Center, many of whom worked closely with children who were affected by the 9/11 attacks, state that a child's reactions will vary depending on a number of factors including age, developmental level, and personality. In the wake of traumatic events, behaviors to expect in our children may include:

- irritability or difficulty being calmed and soothed;
- tearfulness, sadness, and talking about scary ideas or feelings;
- anger directed toward specific communities or ethnic groups;
- fighting or not being able to get along with peers, parents, or other adults;
- changes in sleep patterns, nightmares, or waking in the night;
- wanting to stay close to parents or refusing to go to school; and
- physical complaints such as stomachaches, headaches, or changes in toileting habits.

Children who have experienced recent periods of trauma or family loss or have long-standing emotional problems will be most vulnerable during periods of new threats. This fact only reinforces the idea that we must constantly monitor the media to which our kids are exposed, and be alert for changes in their behavior.

Dr. Steven Marans, the director of the National Center for Children Exposed to Violence at Yale University, has recently written a book entitled *Listening to Fear: Helping Kids Cope, from Nightmares to the Nightly News* in which he provides ways for parents to better understand the emotional landscape of childhood fears. In particular, he asks parents to first begin to work through their own fears; set aside their ideas about what their children are feeling and learn from the children themselves; and third, understand that children and adolescents are likely to communicate their problems using action, so adults and parents must learn to interpret this behavioral language.

POST-TRAUMATIC STRESS DISORDER

From time to time, you may hear the term "post-traumatic stress disorder" (PTSD) used by mental-health professionals to explain or diagnose the symptoms displayed by a child after a catastrophic event. Essentially, PTSD is defined as a severe reaction to trauma.

In the past, PTSD was primarily linked with behaviors displayed by adults who had lived through life-threatening situations, often witnessing death and losing their sense of safety in the world—most often war veterans and survivors of rape. Since the 9/11 attacks, however, mental-health professionals have been startled at the rise of PTSD symptoms in American children, particularly those in New York City. In fact, Dr. Christina Hoven of the National Center for Disaster Preparedness at Columbia University has estimated that 10.5 percent of New York City schoolchildren are suffering from PTSD.

It is important to note that children may display symptoms of PTSD not just in response to a terrorist act or perceived future threat, but in response to any number of events: violent acts such as school shootings, sexual or physical abuse, or motor vehicle accidents, to name but a few.

When experiencing post-traumatic effects, a child may not display immediate symptoms. Moreover, some children may exhibit symptoms of PTSD even when they have not been directly exposed to a trauma. Every child is different. For example, one study conducted soon after the Oklahoma City bombings showed that some children who were not directly exposed to the trauma and who were not related to any victims nonetheless displayed significant PTSD symptoms.

On the other hand, some children may suffer no negative effects from a trauma, while others may try to mask their feelings and will take longer to exhibit noticeable symptoms. Again, every child is different. That is why it is extremely important that we spend quality time with our children after they return from school, day care, or weekend romps with their friends. We know our children best, and will be able to quickly notice changes in their behavior—changes that can be early warning signs of large, long-term problems.

If you do notice changes in your child's mood or behavior, it is always a good idea to consult a licensed mental health professional. If your child is experiencing behavioral problems, the help that you will seek will differ depending on the symptoms he or she displays. For example, minor developmental difficulties may require the services of a school psychologist or counselor, who will make referrals as needed. School psychologists work either in schools or at the district level to help students, parents, and teachers get to the bottom of temporary or long-term learning and behavioral problems. A child psychologist is especially helpful when the behaviors warrant further attention. Psychologists are trained to evaluate and treat your child.

In some cases, particularly when your child's behavior disrupts his or her daily routine for a long period of time, he or she might require the services of a child psychiatrist—a medical doctor trained to help prevent, diagnose, and treat mental, emotional, and behavioral disorders. A psychiatrist will examine your child and make a determination as to whether your child may benefit from medication in addition to concurrent counseling therapy or not.

Choosing the right professional to help your child through his or her period of adjustment is a process that should be taken very seriously. In addition to speaking with your child's pediatrician or health care professional to obtain appropriate referrals, you should consult with the counselor or nurse at your child's school.

Sometimes, short- or long-term medication can be helpful in mediating the effects of PTSD; for this reason, your counselor may want to work with a child psychiatrist to determine the best treatment for your child. In treating PTSD, medication is usually prescribed on a short-term basis; it can cause a reduction in stress reactions and give your child a sense of calm—but, again, this is something you should discuss only with a licensed psychiatrist. Additional tips on choosing the right mental-health services for your child can be found on the Web site of the National Child Traumatic Stress Network at *http://www.nctsnet.org.* (See "Resources" at the end of this book.)

MEMORIES AND MEMORIALS

While professionals remind us that memorials and anniversaries of tragic events are an important part of the healing process, our children may experience them differently. It is important to realize that anniversaries or memorial events can bring up unpleasant memories for children—especially those children who were directly affected by the event being memorialized. Children who have lost friends, parents, or other close relatives may not want to attend such events, because they may bring up old fears and concerns. When considering whether or not your children should attend an anniversary or memorial event—at their school, for example, or at the site of a disaster, or in response to another traumatic event such as the death of a classmate—here are some points to keep in mind:

- **Obtain information about what will take place at the memorial.** This is especially important if the event being memorialized holds particular meaning for your child—if, for example, the child's parent died or was injured in the event.

- **Be mindful of expectations about the day and its meaning.** The significance of the day may provoke complicated emotions. Relief when the day is over may be mixed with further realization of all that has happened in the past year and how different life has become. Not only will the day bring remembrances of a person who died, it can also stir up feelings and reactions related to the event itself. Such an "anniversary reaction"—in which there is a re-experiencing of similar thoughts and emotions from the original tragedy—is not unusual.

- **Plan ahead for the day.** Include everyone involved with the event—colleagues, children, and parents—in your decision making. Discuss the individual thoughts, concerns, ideas, and feelings of everyone involved. Respect everyone's wishes as much as possible. Children, parents, grandparents, friends, teachers, and staff may all have their own needs and ways of coping with difficult events. Some people may be thoughtful and sad, some may want to talk about happy memories, others may want to avoid reminders of the date, prepare elaborate remembrance activities, or stick to a familiar routine and surroundings. Plan activities and events that provide structured options for people with different choices.

- **Consider how different options for memorialization fit your needs.** If the event being memorialized was a public one, as was the case with the 9/11 attacks, there will likely be many options. Decide if you prefer to be part of a large public gathering or engage in a more private event, if you want to be involved in traditional ceremonies such as a community service, or something more personal. Anniversaries provide the chance to decrease isolation, feel supported by those who have had a similar experience, and perhaps appreciate positive outcomes such as renewed community spirit or stronger religious faith.

- Remember that even those who are "doing fine"—that is, adjusting to the aftermath of a trauma or death—may still experience troubling thoughts or feelings. Upsetting feelings about other events or problems from the past may also become evident when a person experiences thoughts or memories of a trauma.

- Be with friends and family, and use all resources available. Those who have previously been a source of support will appreciate being asked to help again, and can provide comfort and assistance—be it a shoulder to cry on or company during a difficult car ride. Enlist the help of others to be "on call" if you need them, or as a help to children in your care if things begin to feel unmanageable.

- Be prepared for changes. Plans may be made, but as the day of a memorial event draws closer, feelings may change. Be flexible, and keep in mind that it may become necessary to make new plans.

- Be calm and supportive. Model healthy expressions of feelings and control.

- Limit media. Viewing repeated images from the past and hearing stories about how others are coping with their grief can be painful and trigger difficult reactions—such as a re-experiencing of past symptoms—or provoke new anxiety and stress related to the trauma.

- Emphasize how new relationships and exciting new opportunities may now become a part of one's life. As time goes by, children, parents, and other family members confront new challenges and realize that things have changed. This is a normal part of the ebb and flow of the bereavement process. Some may need help getting through a rough patch, gaining perspective on events, managing still-troubling feelings, or simply talking things over. If events or feelings seem to interfere with everyday activities, it may help to seek out a professional.

(Source: New York University Child Study Center)

■

Our children feel happy and secure in an environment that gives them the means to express their feelings and curiosity. As parents, we can make this new world that we live in a more secure one for our children by remembering that they are not "little adults" and that they have special needs. Providing our children with the services and resources they need will help them feel safe and secure, even in the midst of a world plagued by terrorism. This is easier said than done, I realize. But the more you are aware of your own feelings, responses, and mental-health status, the better you will be able to care for your child.

CHAPTER 8

MANAGING STRESS

Relaxation as Preparedness

If you are traveling with
a small child or anyone who needs
special assistance, please secure
your own mask first,
place it on your face,
breathe normally,
and then assist your child.
—Airline industry in-flight instructions

THE THREAT OF TERRORISM and global violence has added stress to our already-stressful lives. Every event that could have been explained away before 9/11 as an accident or as happenstance must now filter through a "terrorism sieve"—that is, become the subject of intense scrutiny to determine whether it has anything to do with terrorism. An accident that occurred in November of 2001 provides a compelling example.

On the morning of Veterans Day 2001, reports began flashing across my television screen about an airplane crash that had occurred in the Far Rockaway section of Queens, New York. Far Rockaway sits directly in the takeoff and landing paths of planes using Kennedy Airport, so initial reports of a crash were not unusual. But because this crash occurred only two months and a day after September 11th, New Yorkers and the nation at large were immediately gripped with fear—fear that terrorists had struck again, that they had terrorized us once again on our soil.

The subsequent investigation ruled out terrorism as the cause of the crash, instead attributing it to possible mechanical failure. But the initial public and governmental response to this event clearly illustrated our society's newfound tendency to regard all catastrophic events as potential acts of terrorism. This tendency is accompanied by what I refer to as "sensory overload": a new habit of taking in everything around us, of looking around at everyone and everything, just in case something is amiss or related to a potential act of terrorism.

Now, even years after 9/11, we respond anxiously whenever a plane gets too close to the White House. Several times in the past few years, simple instances of pilot error have triggered "level red" in Washington, D.C.—a heightened state of alert indicating that a terrorist attack is under way and resulting in the temporary relocation of the President, Vice-President, and their families to undisclosed locations; the mass evacuation of thousands of employees and tourists from the Capitol, the Supreme Court, and the White House; and the scrambling of Air Force fighter jets to engage the errant aircraft.

While the prudence of these reactions—and the mass evacuations that followed—will be endlessly debated, one thing is clear: From errant planes in D.C. to suicide bombings in Iraq and the killings of civilian American hostages, unexpected events in the post-9/11 world create high levels of stress for Americans all across the country.

All of this ambient stress, in turn, adds up to bad health, insomnia, irritability, and escalating fear. The reality is that the stressors of life aren't going to go away; the world is only getting more complex. With this in mind, this chapter focuses on stress management—strategies for easing the stress and anxiety associated with uncertain times—as an important form of preparedness.

FACING OUR ANXIETIES

It took me more than two years to realize that I had not taken proper steps to deal with my emotions in response to 9/11. It's not as if I didn't have the opportunity; after all, professional resources had been made available to all New York City employees, especially those of us who were first responders. I simply had not chosen to seek any help. I guess I was exhibiting that silly macho mentality that most men harbor, particularly those of us who work in law enforcement and public safety—the mentality that says we can handle anything.

It wasn't until March of 2004 that I realized I was bottling up my frustrations and emotions regarding the events of September 11th— so much so that I was doing a huge disservice to myself and my family. This revelation occurred while I was attending a Department of Justice training session in Savannah, Georgia. At the seminar,

Dr. Robert (Bob) McGlenn, a friend and noted psychologist who has responded to many disasters and traumas at schools across the country, asked if he could interview me for a book he was writing. As part of the process, he asked to speak with me about my response to the events of 9/11 and how the attacks had affected my life and my family. I agreed, and Bob and I began a talk that initially seemed relaxed and informal, but ultimately forced me to deal with a hidden secret.

As we discussed my first reactions to the attacks and the steps I had taken to ensure the safety of the students and staff of the New York City public schools, I began to speak briefly about how I had almost lost my wife, Kim, during the collapse of the World Trade Center towers. I told Bob how I had dropped Kim at police headquarters in lower Manhattan—only to hear later that she had been sent to the World Trade Center to assist with crowd control and evacuation, and later that she had narrowly escaped death by running at full speed from the collapsing towers. Three years after the event, as I recounted this story to Bob, I began to cry.

After I regained my composure and finished the interview, Bob asked me a very revealing question: "Gregory, how often have you told this story? Have you spoken with any professionals regarding your experiences with 9/11?" I realized that I had not told my story to many people—but when I did, I always got choked up or cried. And of course, true to that macho mentality I referenced earlier, I had not spoken with any professionals about my experiences on 9/11.

Shifting from "friend mode" to "psychologist mode," Bob explained that when we fail to speak about negative experiences in our lives—when we bury them deep inside—we increase our chance of having emotional responses when we are reminded of these experiences later. Bob also said that we increase our potential for emotional and health problems when we allow the stressors of life—work, family, finances (or the lack thereof)—to pile up on top of our repressed feelings.

Lastly, Bob pointed out that speaking with someone—professionals, friends, or family—about the problems in our lives can go a long way toward helping us have a "cleaner plate" that allows us to deal successfully with new things that pop up in our lives. We all lead busy, hectic lives—especially if we are parents, grandparents, or caretakers of loved ones. Each day we begin the hectic process of getting ourselves ready for work, feeding and dressing the kids, packing their lunches, and getting them off to school. Then we go to work where we endure days filled with meetings, deadlines, and personalities that test the limits of our patience. Later, after picking up the kids from one of a dozen after-school activities and cooking them dinner, we watch the evening news on television. In other words, after a long and stressful day, how do many of us choose to unwind? By watching TV reports about war, the threat of terrorism, and unrest and unhappiness around the world.

No wonder we're all so stressed out! The question is, with all this stress, how can we manage it?

DON'T MANAGE STRESS; MASTER IT

Stress is often provoked by a sense of emotional and/or physical danger, powerlessness, or inability to cope with and understand a situation. If we think that a threatening situation has passed, then our nervous system helps to restore us to a general state of balance.

Unfortunately, many of us see the days of our lives as unrelentingly stressful. But unless we find ways to reduce the number of things that "stress us out," the long-term effects on our bodies could be significant, with symptoms ranging from a weakened immune system and rise in blood pressure to hypertension, headaches, muscle fatigue, digestive problems, dizziness, and insomnia.

My friend and colleague Dr. Paula A. Madrid of the National Center for Disaster Preparedness at Columbia University has spent countless hours providing psychotherapy to children, parents, and families directly affected by the 9/11 attacks. Her research and experience inform this chapter, including the following tips for helping you to reduce your general stress levels.

Acknowledge that Some Stress Is Good

The word *stress* didn't always have such a negative connotation. Originally, *stress* was nothing more than an engineering term used to refer to mechanical forces acting on physical structures. It was not until the 1920s that physiologist Walter Cannon first used the term *stress* to refer to the way that our bodies respond to negative or unpleasant conditions.

Having *stress* in our lives can actually be a good thing—provided we learn to cope appropriately. We have grown accustomed to blaming *stress* for our negative feelings, thoughts, and behaviors. But stress should not necessarily be seen as a bad thing. In fact, *good* stress—also called *eustress*, from the Latin *eu*, meaning "good"—is positive and helpful precisely because it is not experienced on a continuous basis. When we do experience good stress, it can help us to focus our energy on completing and dealing with short-term tasks, such as:

- Giving a presentation or speech before a large audience of your peers;
- Meeting your in-laws for the first time;
- Buying a new home or car;
- Getting ready for an important job interview; or even
- Explaining to your husband or wife how you got that large dent in the brand-new family car . . . exactly one day after the warranty ran out!

On the other hand, Dr. Archibald Hart, former Dean of the Graduate School of Psychology at Fuller Theological Seminary, explains, if our bodies continue to experience stress—even "good" stress—

without the chance to return to a normal state of rest and recovery, the result will be "bad" stress (or "distress," from the Latin *dis* meaning "bad"). Take a minute to think about some situations or demands that make you feel stressed out. Are they creating good stress or bad stress?

Know Your Personal Tolerance for Stress

In order to help you recognize whether you are under too much stress, ask yourself the following questions:

- Do you often feel tired or fatigued?
- Do you get colds more than a couple of times a year?
- Are you having more accidents or misplacing objects lately?
- Has decision making become difficult for you—that is, are you asking for lots of advice and making fewer decisions on your own?
- Do you often put the needs of others before your own?
- Do you feel the need to smoke, drink alcohol, or take drugs in order to cope?
- Do you find that you have a hard time enjoying yourself and being generally content?
- Do you find yourself regularly yelling at your children, spouse, or significant other?
- Do you overeat/undereat regularly, and then feel guilty about it afterwards?
- Do you no longer take pride in your appearance?
- Do you feel tearful frequently without always knowing why?

If you answered "yes" to four or more of the questions listed above, you may be suffering from stress overload. Positive answers to some of the questions above may also be an indication of depression. While depression is beyond the scope of this chapter, it is important to remember that any symptom representing a marked difference from your prior levels of functioning, or interfering with your ability to function as expected, may warrant further attention. Stress and depression go hand in hand, and as such need to be recognized quickly so that an action plan can be implemented. Read on for more ways to reduce your stress and live a healthier life.

Eat Well

Studies show that eating balanced, nutritious meals will help you feel vital and strong. It makes sense: Have you ever tried to tackle an important task at work or at home after eating, say, a double-layered Angus cheeseburger with french fries and all the extras?

Nutrition is an essential part of healthful living. Balanced meals and adequate nutrients will give your body energy and your mind a sense of well-being and mastery. You'll think more positive thoughts, feel better about yourself, and have a lot more vitality.

Examples of some especially good-for-you foodstuffs include:

- B–complex vitamins (found in tuna, peanuts, and kidney beans), which may ease depression, and improve cardiovascular health and immunity;
- iron (found in meat, molasses, and spinach), which helps memory and gives you energy;
- thiamin (found in soybean products, sunflower seeds, and peanuts), which can help you feel calm, sleep well, and fight depression;
- carbohydrates, which can calm you down and provide you with energy (though they won't help you lose weight). The healthier sources of carbohydrates are those that are less processed, such as whole wheat, whole grain, etc., or healthy comfort food such as sweet potatoes, minestrone soup, or sautéed vegetables over brown rice;
- low-fat proteins (including meat, fish, and low-fat dairy products), which also provide you with energy;

- green tea, which contains more antioxidants than any other food or beverage and can significantly reduce stress. Antioxidants neutralize free radicals, which are groups of atoms in the body that can damage body cells. Green tea is also thought to help prevent cancer; and

- chocolate, which can be quite stress-relieving when consumed in moderation. One of the major ingredients in chocolate is cacao liquor polyphenol (CLP), a powerful antioxidant that enhances the activity of the immune system.

Also, keep in mind that excess quantities of fatty foods can slow you down and make you feel sluggish.

Sleep Well

Before the light bulb was invented, people slept an average of ten hours per night. Today, Americans average 6.9 hours of sleep on weeknights and 7.5 hours per night on weekends. Getting enough hours of restful, uninterrupted sleep is essential for good health, both physical and emotional.

Even occasional sleeping problems can increase our stress levels and make us less productive. In a recent survey by the National Sleep Foundation, those who said they had trouble getting enough sleep reported greater difficulty concentrating, accomplishing required tasks, and handling minor irritations. Here are a few tips that you should keep in mind in order to improve the quality of your sleep:

- Avoid caffeine, nicotine, and alcohol in the late afternoon and evening. Caffeine and nicotine can interfere with falling asleep, and alcohol may interrupt your sleep later in the night—or make you feel lousy in the morning, which can make you wish you hadn't had that nightcap in the first place.

- If you have trouble sleeping when you go to bed at night, don't nap during the day, as napping can affect your ability to fall asleep later.

- Establish a regular, relaxing bedtime routine that will allow you to unwind and will send a "signal" to your brain that it's time to sleep. Avoid exposure to bright light before bedtime. Hot baths have been known to relax our bodies and speed up the sleep process. Personally, I am also a huge fan of late-night massages!

- Consider your sleep environment. Try your best to make it as pleasant, comfortable, and quiet as you can. If you can't fall asleep after lying in bed for thirty minutes, don't stay in bed tossing and turning. Get up and involve yourself in a relaxing activity, such as listening to soothing music, reading, or watching paint dry until you feel sleepy. Try to clear your mind; don't use this time to worry about your daily problems.

Exercise Regularly

Research has shown that in addition to aiding in the loss of weight and body mass, regular exercise can improve your overall mood and reduce stress. It is generally recommended that every able-bodied person engage in physical activity at least three times per week—to reduce both the chances of succumbing to heart disease and the amount of bone loss that can come with age, often leading to osteoporosis.

It is also recommended that so-called weekend or nighttime athletes spread their physical activity over a number of days, rather than exercising three or four days in a row. Engaging in an activity on consecutive days could increase your chances of injury due to muscle fatigue or overuse. And before you engage in any physical activity, take it from a former collegiate 400-meter man: *Be sure to warm up and stretch those muscles.* Too many injuries occur because tight muscles have not been given the proper warm-up for the stress they are about to undergo.

And when you do exercise, do it at least three hours before bedtime. A workout any later could actually keep you awake, because your body won't have had a chance to cool down. Late-night exercise could also cause marital problems or complaints from the neighbors. One last very important tip: Before you begin any athletic activity, long- or short-term, be sure to see your doctor! It is important to know the amount of stress that your body can handle, and a routine physical will provide you and your doctor with the important information that you need before beginning your exercise program.

Focus on Happy Events and Memories

Think back to your childhood. I'm sure you have a vivid memory of something that truly excited you—of a time when you were really looking forward to something. Maybe you received a special gift from your parents or from that boy or girl you had a crush on in fifth-grade math class. Maybe you were looking forward to a special holiday or a summer vacation. How did the anticipation make you feel? Do you remember your mood at the time, your facial expressions? Try to connect with that feeling whenever you can; put yourself in situations that rekindle those positive feelings. Looking forward to a pleasurable event can be a very effective way of managing stress.

For me, watching shows like *Bugs Bunny* or *The Little Rascals* brings me back to a time when I had no fear of terrorism, no bills to pay, no long hours at work, and no sidewalks or driveways to shovel—unless I was getting paid some serious cash for doing it! Finding those things that make you smile is an effective way of reducing stress. Think about your youth or some of the funniest things you've ever done. Can you find a way to re-create those good times now?

Give Yourself Credit

Focus on the positive aspects of yourself, your life, your friends, and your family—not on the negative aspects or what-ifs. Do you own a house? Are your children healthy? Do you receive E-mails from friends and family? Are you employed? Did you recently meet with your friend for coffee and have a blast? These are all good things. No matter how bleak things look, remind yourself that life does have its happy moments.

Sometimes it helps to keep a journal of all the things for which we feel grateful. To start, take inventory of all the things you *like* about yourself and your life. In addition, resist the urge either to procrastinate or to view projects in your life as absolutely critical and urgent. Instead, experts believe it is best to work on things in moderation—to anticipate situations and prepare for them to avoid stress later on.

It could be that you love cooking while listening to music. If this works for you, why not do it? Or perhaps you like talking on the phone with friends or family, or going for a walk. Arrange your time so you have something to look forward to each day. And try to vary your routine whenever you can. This can be as simple as sitting at a different table in your favorite restaurant, trying a different food or drink, or listening to a new radio station while you're stuck in traffic. The point is to keep your mind active and engaged, which will increase your general sense of well-being.

Try "Thought Switching"

A technique known as "thought switching" has also been found to help manage stress. To practice thought switching, keep a mental catalogue of relaxing places or events that you can "switch on" whenever you feel stressed. Try visualizing a positive memory or fantasy: a favorite beach, a party, an achievement, a peaceful place or time, or a good friend. These positive memories will help you to displace negative or stressful thoughts when they arise.

Many of us are fortunate enough to know exactly what we need to do to reduce our stress levels. For me, reducing stress means going for a two-mile run after work or jumping on my road bike for a long ride. Or it could just mean listening to smooth jazz from saxophonists like David Sanborn or Kirk Walhum. For some people, hobbies can have a calming effect. For others, engaging in hobbies may no longer be as easy as it was when they were younger—for these people, it may be time to explore new activities that can help with stress management.

Keep a Journal

Many people who keep journals on a consistent basis describe journaling as a powerful way to relieve stress. Note that it is not always necessary to keep your journal in diary form. Some people feel stuck when they need to describe the events of their day or their feelings. If this is true for you, consider some other topics:

- Interesting quotations from people, advertisements, or books;
- A timeline of your life;
- A poem;
- Various types of lists: things you want, things you need, things you can't live without, things you'd buy if you were a millionaire, and so on;
- Humorous incidents, jokes, or anecdotes;
- Special moments spent with your family or stories that you'd like your children or grandchildren to know when they grow up;
- Important dates in your child's development; or
- Self-reflective insights about yourself.

Organize Your Life

Another proven way to reduce stress is to avoid rushing things or doing them at the last minute. Try getting up fifteen minutes earlier in the morning; it will make the inevitable morning mishaps—such as not being able to find matching socks . . . been there, done that—seem less stressful.

Most of us really enjoy the extra five minutes of sleep that a snooze alarm can give us. It just seems to be human nature: When we know that we have to get up, we want to sleep more. However, an extra ten to fifteen minutes of appropriately used time in the morning can make a significant difference for the rest of your day. Make a list of all of the little hassles you'd like to avoid in the morning: unexpected traffic, that last-minute phone call, the coffee spill on your shirt, the family member whose extra half hour in the bathroom makes everyone late. Routine can be boring and even stressful at times, but adding a little extra time to your day and establishing a flexible schedule in the morning can give you significant peace of mind. Try to prepare for each morning the evening before. Set the breakfast table, make lunches, put out the clothes you plan to wear, and expect your children to do the same.

Procrastination leads to stress. Whatever you want to do tomorrow, do it today instead; whatever you want to do today, do it now instead! We feel a great deal of stress when we miss important appointments or deadlines. And we're all very busy, so don't rely solely on your memory to remind you of important dates. Try writing down appointment times and locations, and use a portable organizer to remind you about due dates for bills and library books, as well as birthdays and anniversaries (hint for men here!). This is one effective way to prevent stress and also to increase your self-esteem and your sense of efficacy.

The following organizational tips may also help to make your life less stressful:

- Organize your home and workspace so that you always know exactly where things are. If you put things away where they belong, you won't have the stress of losing things and wasting time looking for them.

- When taking care of tedious work around the house, try playing your favorite CD to keep yourself energized.
- Always set up contingency plans, which I like to call "just-in-case" scenarios: for example, "If for some reason either of us is delayed, here's what we'll do . . ." or "If we get split up at the mall, here's where we'll meet . . ." Just-in-case plans can also be helpful as you develop your family emergency plan.
- For once, schedule a realistic day either at work or home. Avoid the tendency to schedule back-to-back appointments. Allow time between appointments to catch your breath.

Take Time for Family and Friends

Make a conscious effort to be a better communicator with your friends and family. Good communication is a key aspect of stress prevention and reduction. Don't be afraid to ask questions, and if you're still not sure about the answers, ask more questions. Taking a few moments to repeat back directions, for example, can prevent stressful miscommunications from occurring later.

Also, learn how to say "no" to things that you know will create undue stress. When we say "no" to extra projects, social activities, and invitations for which we don't have time or energy, it feels good! This takes practice and a belief that we all need quiet time to relax and to be alone. Be sure to share your feelings and concerns with someone whom you trust. Doing this can help dissipate irritability, and helps clear your mind of confusion so you can concentrate on productive problem solving.

Consciously Relax

When we feel stressed, we tend to take short, shallow breaths. When we breathe like this, stale air is not expelled, oxidation of our tissues is incomplete, and muscle tension frequently results. Try to check your breathing patterns throughout the day and before, during, and after high-pressure situations.

If you find that your stomach muscles are knotted and your breathing is shallow, you should try to relax all your muscles and take several deep, slow breaths. When you do this, you will notice that you feel more relaxed, and that both your abdomen and chest will expand when you breathe. You also might want to try the following yoga technique whenever you feel the need to relax: Inhale deeply through your nose and count to eight. Then, with your lips puckered, exhale very slowly through your mouth and count slowly to fifteen. Concentrate on the long sighing sound, and feel the tension dissolve. Repeat this process ten times.

Taking care of our bodies is important. If you feel physically tense, take a hot bath or shower—or a cool one in the summertime—to relieve tension. When you can, treat yourself to a massage or rub lotion on your body. Do something that will improve your appearance; looking better can also help you feel better.

■

All in all, stress—especially the bad kind—can have a cumulative effect on our minds, bodies, and spirits. If we allow stress, anxiety, and depression to take over our lives, we'll find it increasingly difficult to eliminate them. Take time every day to scan yourself, body and mind. Allow time every day for privacy, quiet, and introspection—time to ask yourself: "How do I feel?"; "What do I want?"; "What do I need right now?"; "How happy am I?" The good news is that when you make these daily assessments of your life, you'll find that you have an awful lot to be thankful for.

Afterword

When I agreed to write the afterword for this excellent book written by my colleague and friend, Gregory Thomas, I knew that this would be an important read for all Americans. None of us can escape the sad reality of risk in today's world. Natural disasters and industrial accidents happen, and sometimes they are destructive and deadly.

International terrorism, too, is a part of our world. On that terrible day in September of 2001, a lot changed for our country. For so many of us, an illusion of safety and isolation was shattered along with the twin towers of lower Manhattan. This was a hard introduction to the reality of a world that we once viewed as almost too far away, geographically and conceptually, to worry about. We found out that we were far more vulnerable than we may have thought. It is one thing to absorb the wrath of nature gone wild and powerful, and it's quite another to know firsthand the capacity of human beings who want to kill and terrorize innocent civilians.

It's not that terrorism is unknown on U.S. soil. In fact, since the earliest days of the Republic, we have had our share of irrational violence against civilians. How else could we describe our own behaviors against native American populations in the first one hundred or more years of our nation's history? Or the burning of Southern cities during the civil war? Or the institutionalized brutality against African Americans forcibly brought here and relegated to virtual sub-human status by a society that thought human slavery was an acceptable economic necessity? Or the sheer evil of Timothy McVeigh in Oklahoma City who destroyed the Murrah Federal Building along with the lives of 168 innocent men, women and children?

Still, 9/11 was different. For one thing, it occurred in our own lifetimes, so much more vivid and unsettling than any horrific episode in history could ever be. For another thing, the attacks of that day were planned and executed by people "from without." In fact, we were invaded; violated as well as wounded. This creates a very different sense of vulnerability among most people. But how we cope with vulnerability, and the extent to which it affects our lives and behaviors, ultimately determines whether we're generally resilient—or whether we will live in a state of anxiety, precisely fulfilling the desired goals of international terrorists.

When I began writing this afterword, I was heading home from Baton Rouge, Louisiana after spending time with officials in the Emergency Operations Center for that state. That visit followed several days in Mississippi where I reviewed our own efforts to help survivors of the devastated communities of Biloxi and Gulfport. It had been my second trip to the region.

The timing of these visits was some three weeks after Hurricane Katrina smashed into the Gulf States, but just as preparations were being reviewed for a second large storm, Hurricane Rita. This latest storm seemed to be on a collision course for Galveston and Houston. Ultimately, Rita missed these major population centers and weakened as it made landfall.

But, until it was clear that the cities would not be in significant danger, officials had no choice but to initiate emergency measures, including a full evacuation of Houston—the nation's fourth largest city.

What we saw in the two back-to-back hurricanes was a very mixed bag of emergency preparedness and response. In the case of Katrina, the nation seemed ill-prepared on almost every imaginable score. Social order collapsed. Food, water and emergency medical care was not available. People waited days for rescue from rooftops in flooded neighborhoods, as sick patients from evacuated hospitals waited at the airport until they could be airlifted to safety. And for some, that wait proved fatal. On the large scale, confusion and chaos reigned. It was not clear who was in charge or how decisions were made with respect to calling in Federal assistance. Even the principle non-governmental relief organizations, like the Red Cross and the Salvation Army, seemed all but invisible, especially in those early days immediately after the hurricane and subsequent flooding.

Three weeks later, in Houston, the lessons from Hurricane Katrina seemed to be somewhat absorbed as that city waited for their own killer storm. This time food and water were pre-positioned and National Guard troops were at the ready.

But other official actions seemed disorganized and flawed. An evacuation order was issued for a city that is extraordinarily dependent upon automobiles. For those without cars, busses were pressed into service. But the actual directions were confusing and contradictory. Emergency managers had grossly underestimated the number of vehicles that would be on the road. Traffic flow orders were given, rescinded and given again. And, in an amazing lapse of planning, gasoline was not available for the thousands and thousands of vehicles that jammed the roads, slowing traffic to a painful crawl.

Looking at both of these events, the conclusion was clear: the nation was not prepared to cope with major disasters.

Yet, in many instances involving lesser events, planning for and response to a wide range of disaster scenarios is effective. Large fires, plane crashes, chemical plant explosions and even a suicide bomber in a subway can be managed by well-trained local and state officials. Even the response to the attacks of 9/11/01 seemed organized and under control, in spite of New York City and the whole nation being in a collective state of shock.

The problem arises when the scale and scope of an event overwhelms the resources available locally to respond. It is here that we need to rethink the assumptions of preparedness, evaluate how we plan, and clarify when and how the federal government will be called in. This rethinking will be essential if we are to genuinely improve our ability to save lives in a major disaster.

For individuals and their families, there are other important insights that should be emphasized. None is more important than a basic principle of emergency planning. Effective emergency response is often about a good working relationship among citizens, government and non-governmental relief agencies.

In other words, as Gregory Thomas notes, people affected by or proximal to a disaster are likely to be the first responders—needing to act appropriately and decisively before the police, fire, or other rescue workers arrive. These minutes, hours and days can literally mean life or death.

So how do citizens do their part in the partnership for life in the aftermath of a major disaster? Part of the answer lies in good preparedness planning. And the book covers all of this very well. No matter what, it behooves each of us to familiarize ourselves with the risks we face and the basic means of staying safe before, during, and after a major catastrophic event.

But, obviously, preparing for disasters is not only about what individuals should do. As we watched the response to the storms of September 2005, we couldn't help appreciate how much more government needs to do in order to optimize the chances of people surviving catastrophic events.

First, our government needs to rapidly assess the accomplishments and failures of recent efforts to prepare for and respond to major disasters. We need to understand the lessons learned and we need to catalog the "best practices"—or ideas and plans that worked well under real-time conditions.

Second, we need a system of preparedness that is much more accountable. This starts with defining what we mean by preparedness, describing how we get there and demanding real accountability from those who are spending tax dollars on disaster preparedness.

Third, we have to establish a much improved system for command and control in major emergencies. How do the agencies report to one another? And, who's calling the shots?

All of these steps would likely improve our ability to withstand a disaster—of any magnitude and from any cause. And, the more we know, the better we get, the more likely it is that loss of life will be as low as it can be, no matter what the circumstances.

Finally, it is worth remembering that preparedness should not become an obsession. We should do what needs to be done prudently and efficiently. This goes for individuals, families, communities and government. At the end of the day, preparedness should be a matter of course and an important factor in making all Americans resilient, resistant to fear and capable of looking at the future with optimism and hope.

Irwin Redlener, M.D.
Associate Dean
Director, The National Center for Disaster Preparedness
Columbia University Mailman School of Public Health

Resources

U.S. Department of Homeland Security (DHS)
http://www.dhs.gov/dhspublic/

Check this site for the status of the Threat Advisory and the latest news on disasters and emergencies. In addition, the DHS provides a compendium of information on preparing for emergencies, including helpful links to resources, as well as excellent guidelines for preparing to travel abroad.

Homeland Security State Contact List
http://www.whitehouse.gov/homeland/contactmap.html

Use this site to find out whom your Governor has appointed as your state's homeland security contact.

Emergency Preparedness Guide for Homeowners
http://www.dhs.gov/

Developed by the U.S. Department of Homeland Security and the Homeownership Alliance, this guide provides homeowners with practical measures they can take to prepare themselves, their families, and their homes for any possible emergencies. The guide includes information on: emergency supplies; effective emergency plans for families; various threats homeowners may face; and resources available to homeowners through the DHS, the Homeownership Alliance, and local government and community officials.

The America Prepared Campaign
http://www.americaprepared.org/

America Prepared supports the work already begun by the Department of Homeland Security's Ready campaign and the American Red Cross—work aimed at giving Americans useful recommendations for preparing their homes and families for terrorist attacks. On this site, you can download a family communications plan and get information on how to purchase or put together an emergency kit. You can also take a quiz to see how ready you really are.

Federal Emergency Management Agency (FEMA)
http://www.fema.gov/

FEMA is charged with helping the United States and its citizens plan for, respond to, recover from, and mitigate against disasters. Besides providing information on active disasters and emergencies, this Web site offers a virtual library of preparation and prevention resources. View PDFs or order printed copies of everything from an "Emergency Preparedness Checklist" to a "Disaster Plan for Families."

DisasterHelp.gov
http://disasterhelp.gov/portal/jhtml/index.jhtml

Established by the President's Management Council, this site offers a compendium of disaster-related resources. Section titles include: "Terrorism Government Resources,"

"Acts of Terror Links," "Animal and Plant Safety," and "America Responds to Terrorism." Though primarily directed toward government leaders and first responders, this site also features many valuable resources.

FireSafety.gov
http://www.firesafety.gov/

On this site, the U.S. Fire Administration provides fact sheets on home fire safety; a kids' page with games and safety tips for children; facts on fire; and an online catalog listing more than two hundred safety-related publications.

American Red Cross
http://www.redcross.org/

Disaster preparedness and mitigation are top priorities of the American Red Cross. Together with FEMA and other partners, the Red Cross is leading efforts across the nation to do more before disasters strike, to build a "culture of prevention," and to limit the harm inflicted on families and communities. Visit the Red Cross Web site to learn more about these efforts, as well as to find practical tips on preparedness. In addition, the Red Cross has created the Together We Prepare initiative, which offers guidelines organized into the following topics: making a plan, building a kit, getting trained, volunteering, giving blood, and pledging to prepare.

Ready.gov
http://www.ready.gov/useful_state.html

Visit this link to the U.S. Department of Homeland Security's Ready.gov site for an overview of state agencies that can provide emergency-related assistance.

Center for Trauma Response, Recovery & Preparedness (CTRP)
http://www.ctrp.org/

Based in Connecticut, the CTRP has worked to develop a behavioral-health crisis plan that addresses the needs of children and adults in the event of natural or man-made disasters. It has formed five Behavioral Health Regional Crisis Response Teams that provide time-limited crisis intervention services to affected individuals and communities. In addition, the CTRP is currently working to reach out to public health and emergency response teams, firefighters, police, health providers, schools, clergy, and others to systematically address local behavioral-health needs in times of crisis. Visit the Web site for links to educational materials and other resources geared specifically to families, educators, first responders, and more. Or call (860) 679-8790 for more information.

The 9/11 Commission Report: Final Report of the National Commission on Terrorist Attacks Upon the United States
by *National Commission on Terrorist Attacks*
W. W. Norton & Company; Authorized edition (July 22, 2004)

Exhaustively researched and compiled by a specially appointed bipartisan council, *The 9/11 Commission Report* is a thorough and instructive account of the events of September 11, 2001. Given full access to a staggering collection of evidence, the panel reveals the origins of al Qaeda and the details of their attack plan, and lays bare the errors in intelligence-gathering and defense that helped facilitate al Qaeda's actions.

Going beyond the day of the attack, the panel arrives at a series of tough questions regarding the future of national security and recommends a series of measures designed to strengthen the safety of our country.

RESOURCES FOR PARENTS

National School Safety Center (NSSC)
http://www.nssc1.org/

An advocate for safe and secure schools, the NSSC provides a variety of information and resources. Recent articles posted to the Web site include: "Managing Schools Under the Threat of Terrorism," "The Role of Schools in Homeland Security," "School Safety Assessment," and "Working Together to Create Safe Schools" (free handout).

National Center for Post-Traumatic Stress Disorder
http://www.ncptsd.org/index.html

Visit this Web site for information on post-traumatic stress disorder (PTSD), including effects and possible reactions to traumatic situations. In addition, the site offers guidelines for recognizing PTSD symptoms and offers coping-skills training.

American Psychological Association (APA)
http://www.apa.org/topics/topictrauma.html

The APA site offers a range of information on everything from post-traumatic stress syndrome warning signs to suggestions for combating terrorism. In addition, it provides guidelines for children, links to other resources, and a toll-free number that you can call for help in finding a psychologist.

National Child Traumatic Stress Network (NCTSN)
http://www.nctsnet.org/

This site provides resources about child traumatic stress for parents, school personnel, media, and other professionals. NCTSN is dedicated to improving care and access to services for children who have been traumatized, their families, and their communities. It provides practical information and resources about child traumatic stress, as well other related topics.

SAMHSA National Mental Health Information Center
http://www.mentalhealth.samhsa.gov/

The National Mental Health Information Center was developed for users of mental-health services and their families, the general public, policy makers, providers, and the media. Information Center staff members are skilled at listening and responding to questions from the public and from professionals. Call (800) 789-2647 or visit the Web site.

National Center for Children Exposed to Violence (NCCEV)
http://www.nccev.org/

This site provides resources, training, and a bibliographic database. The NCCEV seeks to increase public and professional awareness of the effects of violence on children, as well as to extend the capacity of individuals and communities to reduce the incidence and impact of violence. A primary national resource center, the NCCEV provides information about the effects of violence on children and initiatives addressing these issues, including a dynamic body of literature and Internet resources. To view these resources and to learn more about this organization, visit the Web site or call (877) 49-NCCEV.

Sesame Street Workshop

http://www.sesameworkshop.org/youcanask/

Developed by Sesame Workshop, this Web site includes a section on parenting advice and a section called "You Can Ask!" that is devoted to helping three- to eight-year-olds build social and emotional skills as well as cope with whatever comes their way.

Heroic Choices

http://www.heroicchoices.org/

Originally the Todd M. Beamer Foundation, Heroic Choices is a nonprofit youth services organization that builds resiliency in children who have experienced trauma. Its twelve-month program supports children, families, and mentors. This free program targets children ages eight to twelve who have experienced trauma, which may include but is not limited to: the loss of a parent, guardian, relative, or friend; domestic violence; physical or sexual abuse; drug or alcohol abuse in the home; and parental incarceration. For more information, visit the Web site or call (866) HERO-111.

SITES FOR CHILDREN

KidsHealth!

http://www.kidshealth.org/kid/

This Web site provides doctor-approved health information about children from before birth through adolescence. Created by The Nemours Foundation's Center for Children's Health Media, this site offers accurate, up-to-date, and easy-to-understand health information for parents, kids, and teens. It also features special sections on terrorism and war.

FEMA for Kids

http://www.fema.gov/kids/

Operated by the Federal Emergency Management Agency, this site teaches kids how to be prepared for disasters and how to prevent disaster damage. Kids can also learn what causes disasters, play games, read stories, and become "Disaster Action Kids."

American Liberty Partnership

http://www.libertyunite.org/kids.adp

Read examples of how youth took action and played a role in rebuilding our country, and find out how you and your friends can get involved in your community.

FirstGov for Kids

http://www.kids.gov/

This site was developed and is maintained by the Federal Citizen Information Center. It provides links to federal kids' sites, along with some of the best kids' sites from other organizations, all grouped by subject.

USFA Kids Page American Academy

http://www.usfa.fema.gov/kids/

Operated by the United States Fire Administration, the Kids Page is full of tips that can help children and their families be safe from fire. Learn more about escape planning, home fire safety, and smoke alarms. Kids can also enjoy games and become "Junior Fire Marshals."

RESOURCES ABOUT CHILDREN

American Academy of Pediatrics

Children, Terrorism & Disasters

http://www.aap.org/terrorism/index.html

The American Academy of Pediatrics, an organization composed of pediatricians and specialists dedicated to the health and safety of infants, children and young persons, established its national Task Force on Terrorism after the events of 9/11. This Web site for the Task Force's section on Children, Terrorism & Disasters offers links for teachers, parents, and community planners to learn about disaster preparedness, especially for families and children dealing with crisis and tragedy. Also included are useful links to information about topics such as biological and chemical agents, psychosocial aspects, and public policy, as well as links to other resourceful Web sites about children and disaster preparedness.

American Academy of Child & Adolescent Psychiatry

http://www.aacap.org/publications/DisasterResponse/index.htm

Presented in both English and Spanish, this Web site was established after the 2005 school shooting in Minnesota to offer families information about disaster response and prevention. Links to such topics as Understanding Violent Behavior in Children and Adolescents and Helping Children After a Disaster provide information on recognizing children's issues as well as some suggestions on what steps to take. This Web site is part of the AACAP's *Facts for Families*, which provides information for families on a variety of children's issues, including Children and Firearms, Conduct Disorder, and Child Sexual Abuse, many of which are also available in French or Polish.

"Talking to Children about Terrorism and War"

http://www.aacap.org/publications/factsFam/87.htm

Also a publication of AACAP's *Facts for Families*, this Web site gives detailed advice on talking to children about terrorism and war, but many of the tips can be applied to any disaster or crisis situation. On this Web site you will find help for listening to children, answering children's questions, and providing support.

U.S. Department of Health and Human Services: Administration for Children and Families

http://www.acf.hhs.gov/acf_about.html

The mission of the Administration for Children and Families is to provide federal programs that promote the social and economic well-being of individuals, families, children, and communities. The Web site outlines information about the many services that the ACF provides or helps families with, including adoption and foster care, child support, Head Start, and many others. There is also information on this site about working with the ACF in your own community as well as policies and facts about the ACF itself.

Connect for Kids

http://www.connectforkids.org

Based in Washington, D.C., Connect for Kids is a resource for adults to help improve the lives of children and families. There are an extensive number of topics and subtopics with information for adults to choose from, as well as guides and other types of content, such as articles, field reports, and tool kits. This Web site is a good tool for adults who play any role in children's lives, be they parents, educators, policy makers, or others, and there is information and help pertaining to children of all ages.

information they should have prior to such a situation. Tips on what to keep in a disaster kit and who to call in the event of an emergency are provided, as well as what types of items are unnecessary and even potentially dangerous. At the end of the piece is a useful link to another article that offers advice on developing disaster plans for older and distant relatives.

The Red Cross

Disaster Preparedness for Seniors by Seniors

http://www.redcross.org/services/disaster/beprepared/seniors.html

This Web site contains an abundance of important information for senior citizens on how to prepare for disasters and deal with them, before, during, and after. From medical needs to shelter to evacuation, the information on this Web site is practical and valuable for all types of crises and disasters. Links on the site lead to preparation advice for specific situations, many of which, like this site, are available in a large selection of foreign languages.

RESOURCES FOR SENIORS

AARP

http://www.aarp.org/bulletin/yourlife/Articles/a2003-06-26-protecting.html

This link will take you to an article on the American Association of Retired Persons' Web site about the special needs of elderly citizens in the event of a terrorist attack and its aftermath. With the emphasis on preparation, the article warns about the possibilities of elderly people being left to take care of themselves for a few days after an attack, and what materials and

RESOURCES FOR PEOPLE WITH DISABILITIES

City of Los Angeles Emergency Preparedness Handbook for Persons with Disabilities

http://www.lacity.org/dod/handbook.pdf

This link opens a PDF file of the *Preparedness Handbook for Persons with Disabilities* as presented by the City of Los Angeles, but is comprehensive and suitable for people with disabilities living in any part of the country. The handbook is a good resource for important things to keep in a home and items to have in a kit in case of an emergency, as well as general information on making your home itself safer and more prepared. Chapters are separated categorically and include "For People Who Are Blind or Have Visual Impairments," "For Owners of Service Animals and Pets," "For People with Mobility Limitations," "For People Who Are Deaf or Hard-of-Hearing," and "For People with Special Medical Needs." While the emergency reference numbers are for Los Angeles only, the "Emergency Information List" and "Medical Information List" are universal and extremely useful.

Easter Seals

s.a.f.e.t.y. first

http://www.easter-seals.org/site/ PageServer?pagename=ntl_safety_first

Easter Seals Disability Services provides help and services to people of all ages with disabilities and special needs and their families. The *s.a.f.e.t.y.first* effort was initiated in response to September 11, 2001, reaching out to all members of communities, especially those that include persons with disabilities. The acronym of the effort's title stands for six tips on how to prepare for an emergency evacuation after a disaster or attack that focuses on the needs of disabled persons. Also found on the *s.a.f.e.t.y.first* site are the "10 Key Considerations for Someone with Special Needs" and support and advice for developing an evacuation plan. As a community-based effort, *s.a.f.e.t.y.first* is a good source of information and planning for everyone, including a downloadable PDF on "tenant safety" as provided by the Building Owners and Managers Association (BOMA).

Emergency Management Institute, FEMA

Emergency Planning and Special Needs Populations course

http://www.training.fema.gov/emiweb/ pub/crsselect.asp

Due to an overwhelming request for enrollment in the Emergency Management Institute's G197 Emergency Planning and Special Needs Population course, they have provided the materials for the course to be downloaded. These materials include an Instructor's Guide, a Student Manual, Visuals, Handouts, and Resources. While these materials are useful and free of charge, they are meant to be used in an instructor-led training and are not intended for self-study and will not result in a certificate of training. Check the Web site for information on classes offered in your state, or contact your State Training Office of Emergency Management.

Center for Disability Issues and the Health Professions

http://www.cdihp.org/

Web site of Western University's CDIHP, dedicated to enhancing health professions education and improving access of people with disabilities to health education and services.

The National Organization on Disability

http://www.nod.org

This Web site is active and updated often, and offers information and resources for and about disabled persons and disability. The site offers a listing of calendars that have information on disability-related events and observances, as well as an E-

Newsletter that can keep you up-to-date on disability news, information, and resources. Other topics on the Web site include community involvement, economic participation, and access to independence.

RESOURCES FOR MENTAL HEALTH

National Mental Health Association
Coping with Disaster

http://www.nmha.org/reassurance/anniversary/index.cfm

With an emphasis on the results of war and terrorism on mental health, the National Mental Health Association presents the Coping with Disaster fact sheet. The Web site provides copious information on all types of people and situations with categories that include "Coping with the Stress of Ongoing Military Operations," "Returning Home from War: Tips for the Troops," "Coping with Terrorism," and "Coping with War." There are also sections designated to help people deal with specific tragedies, such as September 11th and its anniversaries, the *Columbia* Space Shuttle Tragedy, and the Indian Ocean tsunami disaster. A variety of Resources links are also available on the Web site.

Montgomery County, MD
The Healing Project

http://www.montgomerycountymd.gov/mcgtmpl.asp?url=/Content/HealingProj/index.asp

The Healing Project is a cooperative effort between several state and federal organizations, including the Maryland Department of Health and Mental Hygiene and the U.S. Department of Homeland Security, geared toward the identification and treatment of Post-traumatic stress disorder (PTSD). On the Web site, you can view a video about the Healing Project, take a test to identify your own stress, and order free materials about the Healing Project in English or Spanish. Also on the Web site are links to other sites where you can learn more about traumatic stress, such as the Web sites for the National Center for PTSD and the U.S. Department of Health and Human Services.

Health Resources and Service Administration
Rural Communities and Emergency Preparedness

http://ruralhealth.hrsa.gov/initiative.htm

There are four important links on this Web page and they lead to the HHS Rural Task Force Report to the Secretary, Secretary Thompson's Speech at the Summit on Rural America, the Press Release on the Summit on Rural America, and the HHS paper on Rural Communities and Emergency Preparedness. The last is a thorough report on why rural response to disaster is important, what the rural public health infrastructure is, and how rural communities should prepare for emergencies. The report is comprehensive and informative, providing questions that should be addressed for all rural communities and their members.

American Psychiatric Association
http://www.psych.org/

The American Psychiatric Association is the oldest national medical specialty association in America. Its Web site provides information on the group's mission to ensure that all persons with mental health issues receive competent and humane care.

The Red Cross

www.redcross.org

For over a century, the American Red Cross has provided medical and disaster services in America and internationally. The Web site offers a wealth of information on the services the Red Cross provides and how to contribute to those efforts. Easy to navigate, the Red Cross site offers FAQ pages on everything from disasters to nursing to volunteering. You can also sign up for monthly E-mails with news, safety tips, and disaster updates.

The US Department of Homeland Security

http://www.ready.gov/

Aptly named, Ready.gov is the comprehensive Web site of the U.S. Department of Homeland Security designed to prepare Americans for potential terrorist attacks. The main sections provide information on making emergency supply kits, making plans in case of an emergency, and how to stay informed. This last section gives overviews of and information on how to handle varied situations, from biological threats and natural disasters to nuclear blasts and other explosions. Much of what you need to know to be prepared can be found here.

National Institute of Mental Health

http://www.nimh.nih.gov/

Web site of the National Institute of Mental Health, an organization committed to improving mental health through biomedical research. This site offers a variety of information on mental health, from anxiety disorders to autism spectrum disorders to schizophrenia. The Web page also keeps updated information on research and funding, as well as a section for "breaking news" in the mental health field.

(Reprinted with permission of the website of the Families of September 11, Inc. [www.familiesofseptember11.org])

Homeland Security Family Communications Plan

Your family may not be together when disaster strikes, so plan how you will contact one another and review what you will do in different situations.

Out-of-Town Contact Name _____   Telephone Number: _____
Email: _____   Telephone Number: _____

Fill out the following information for each family member and keep it up to date.

Name:	Social Security Number:
Date of Birth:	Important Medical Information:
Name:	Social Security Number:
Date of Birth:	Important Medical Information:
Name:	Social Security Number:
Date of Birth:	Important Medical Information:
Name:	Social Security Number:
Date of Birth:	Important Medical Information:
Name:	Social Security Number:
Date of Birth:	Important Medical Information:
Name:	Social Security Number:
Date of Birth:	Important Medical Information:

Where to go in an emergency. Write down where your family spends the most time: work, school and other places you frequent. Schools, daycare providers, workplaces and apartment buildings should all have site-specific emergency plans.

Home
Address:
Phone Number:
Neighborhood Meeting Place:
Regional Meeting Place:

Work
Address:
Phone Number:
Evacuation Location:

School
Address:
Phone Number:
Evacuation Location:

Work
Address:
Phone Number:
Evacuation Location:

School
Address:
Phone Number:
Evacuation Location:

Other place you frequent:
Address:
Phone Number:
Evacuation Location:

School
Address:
Phone Number:
Evacuation Location:

Other place you frequent:
Address:
Phone Number:
Evacuation Location:

Important Information	Name	Telephone #	Policy #
Doctor(s):			
Other:			
Pharmacist:			
Medical Insurance:			
Homeowners/Rental Insurance:			
Veterinarian/Kennel (for pets):			

Other useful phone numbers: **9–1–1 for emergencies.**   Police Non-Emergency Phone #: _____

Every family member should carry a copy of this important information:

Other Important Phone Numbers & Information:

< FOLD HERE >

🛡 Family Communications Plan

Contact Name:
Telephone:

Out-of-Town Contact Name
Telephone:

Neighborhood Meeting Place:
Meeting Place Telephone:

Dial 9-1-1 for Emergencies!

Other Important Phone Numbers & Information:

🛡 Family Communications Plan

Contact Name:
Telephone:

Out-of-Town Contact Name
Telephone:

Neighborhood Meeting Place:
Meeting Place Telephone:

Dial 9-1-1 for Emergencies!

Other Important Phone Numbers & Information:

< FOLD HERE >

🛡 Family Communications Plan

Contact Name:
Telephone:

Out-of-Town Contact Name
Telephone:

Neighborhood Meeting Place:
Meeting Place Telephone:

Dial 9-1-1 for Emergencies!

Other Important Phone Numbers & Information:

🛡 Family Communications Plan

Contact Name:
Telephone:

Out-of-Town Contact Name
Telephone:

Neighborhood Meeting Place:
Meeting Place Telephone:

Dial 9-1-1 for Emergencies!

Acknowledgments

I can do all things through christ who strengthens me—Philippians 4:13. As I take this time to formally recognize and thank those who helped me take this book from thought to print, I must start first with thanking my Lord and Savior, Jesus Christ. Like the words that are offered in the quote above, from the offer to write this book and throughout the entire process, I knew that I had the strength to finish the work on time and on message. I knew because I can do all things through Christ who strengthens me.

To ensure that I get the acknowledgements right, let me start with the person who approached me with the idea of writing *Freedom from Fear*. The thanks start with Jena Pincott, senior editor for Random House Reference. I remember the day well when Jena called me saying that Random House was interested in publishing a book to help families prepare for emergencies, natural disasters or acts of terrorism and that with the help of her editorial assistant, Laura Neilson (who did the research and the Internet search that came up with my name), she decided to contact me. Jena was a joy to work with and was patient with my role as a first-time solo author. I owe a lot to her for keeping me focused, concise and determined. I am indebted to Jena, Laura, and all of their colleagues at Random House including publisher Sheryl Stebbins, Elizabeth Bennett, William Tracy, Tigist Getachew, Beth Levy, Carolyn Roth and Lisa Montebello. Thank you Random House for trusting that I would "do the right thing" by you. In the end, you surely did the right thing by me!

I owe a lot to my family as well. Let me first thank my parents, Ann and the late Joseph Thomas, for "raising me right" and giving me the proper dose of discipline, love and appreciation for the value of education, all of which came into play as I hunkered down to write this book. On the home front, I must give thanks to my loving wife Kim and my sons Tyler and Joseph. Throughout the process, Kim showed me the way by encouraging me when I hit the "writer's wall" and made sure that I kept my "eyes on the prize". My son Tyler applied his "teenage computer smarts" when I needed to purchase a quality laptop so I could take my writing on the road and also helped me format my manuscript. Joseph, who was miles away in his home in Charlotte, North Carolina and works for a major book distribution firm, offered me encouragement and professional advice from afar. Together, Kim, Tyler, and Joseph all provided me with the time, laughter, support, comfort and *space* that I needed to get the job done while never missing a deadline. I know that I could not have done it without them. Thanks, family!

Two long-time friends helped immensely as I began to write the manuscript. Those friends were Dr. Thomas LaVeist, a professor and Director of the Center for Health Disparities Solutions at the Johns Hopkins Bloomberg School of Public Health, and Michael Dorn, an internationally renowned expert in school safety and security who currently serves as a Senior Consultant for Public Safety and Emergency Management with the Janes Information Group. Thomas, who is my fraternity brother and college classmate, offered many words of wisdom during the development, writing, and marketing phases. Michael, who is the author of over twenty books, provided advice as I conducted research and began to edit my chapters.

The research that Michael conducted with his son Chris for their recent book: *Innocent Targets: When Terrorism Comes to School* helped me greatly as I wrote the chapter on school preparedness. I am indebted to both Thomas and Michael for taking the time out of their busy lives to lend me a hand.

As I began to write and edit the initial drafts of *Freedom from Fear,* I recognized that I needed someone whom I could trust to "read what I wrote" to see if it a) made sense and b) was on topic. I found that person in Elizabeth (Beth) Fuller. Beth and I are colleagues in the National Center for Disaster Preparedness at Columbia University and although she was in the middle of writing her doctoral dissertation, Beth took countless hours out from her already busy life to read, re-read, critique, and edit my manuscripts. She did it with style, sensitivity, grace and most importantly, with humor. Thanks, Beth, for keeping me on message and on mission!

I need to also thank my good friend, Dr. Paula Madrid, who also works with me at the National Center for Disaster Preparedness and serves as the Director of the Resiliency Program. Paula volunteered to offer her thoughts and experiences for the chapter on stress. Paula is another person who has a demanding day and evening as she provides needed mental health support to, amongst others, families of victims of the 9/11 attacks. In spite of all of her other obligations, she found the time to contribute a major chapter to my book. Ola, Paula, *muchos, muchos gracias* for being a great leaning post and a friend!

Dr. Irwin Redlener who is the Director of the National Center for Disaster Preparedness at Columbia University and Associate Dean in the Mailman School of Public Health deserves a special note of thanks as well. Dr. Redlener travels the country and the world to send the message that we all need to "adjust our sails" in the post-9/11 era. He drives that message home through the work that we do everyday at the National Center and through many noted speeches and publications. He agreed to write the afterword for my book where he again shows his passion for preparedness for disasters, whether man-made or natural. Irwin, thanks for providing your vision and thoughts for the future of our nation in the post-9/11 era.

I owe a lot to Dr. Robyn Gershon and Dr. Christina Hoven as well, both of whom are on faculty at the Columbia University Mailman School of Public Health, for their mentorship and for their landmark research that appears in my book. I also owe particular thanks to my good friends Dr. Nancy Degnan, Associate Director of the Columbia University Center for Environmental Research, for keeping me on the straight and narrow through her "spiritual counsel" when times got tough and Yumie Song, friend, colleague and doctoral student at the Columbia University School of International and Public Affairs, for helping define and write to the intended audience. Many words of support could also be found from all my other colleagues at the National Center for Disaster Preparedness at Columbia University. To a person they all offered encouragement and made sure that I kept focused, never letting me lose sight of how important the preparedness message of this book was. I owe you all big time. Thanks, team!

Many other friends and colleagues provided excerpts that made this book both readable and credible. I am indebted to my friend David Ropeik, Director of Risk Communication at the Harvard University Center for Risk Analysis. His widely quoted views on risk and risk perception that appear in my book were proper, easy to understand, and the perfect fit. Thank you David for lending me a steady hand. I must also thank my friends Dr. Lynn Davis and Dr. Bradley Stein and their colleagues from the RAND Corporation, Judy Lewis and Ellen Tunkelrott for helping to provide me with what I call a common sense guide (which appears in the chapter on family preparedness) to help us prepare and respond to terrorist attacks that emanate from weapons of mass destruction (WMD's). My thanks also go out to my friend JoAnn Jordan who is the Education Coordinator for the City of Bellevue Fire Department in Bellevue, Washington for providing her insight and advice for the chapter on school preparedness. The resource section of this book is strong because of the efforts of the staff of the Families of September 11, Inc. (FOS 11). The FOS 11 founders, their Board of Directors and their staff, in particular Executive Director Jennifer Mincin, Caitlin Zampella, and Dan Fiedler all deserve thanks for allowing to reference their hard work. Steven Brill, the Chairman and founder of the America Prepared Campaign (APC) deserves thanks as well for providing me with sound advice as I began to shape the book.

Steve, the APC board of directors, my fellow members of the advisory panel and the entire APC staff also deserve a standing round of applause for being the drive behind the designation of September as National Preparedness Month!

As I bring the acknowledgements to a close, I would be greatly remiss if I did not thank Jim Clifton, the Chairman and CEO of the Gallup Organization, for taking time to review my book. Under Jim's leadership the Gallup Organization conducts timely polls that provide the pulse of Americans related to terrorism and disasters and as such often serve as the impetus for change. Thanks Jim for providing the leadership and for your valued comments about the need for this book. Last but certainly not least, I must thank former Congressman and former Vice Chair of the National Commission on Terrorist Attacks upon the United States (the 9/11 Commission), Lee H. Hamilton, for agreeing to write the foreword for my book. His words and vision set the perfect tone and I along with the readers of it are blessed to be witness to them. Thank you Vice-Chair Hamilton for committing your relevant words to my work. I would be greatly negligent if I did not at this time also thank Philip Duncan, Rita Foy Moss and Ben Rhodes for helping me secure Mr. Hamilton's voice. Ben in particular played a central role as my main point of contact and ensured that Mr. Hamilton's words and vision were properly represented in his foreword. And one last special note of thanks needs to go Mr. Hamilton, the Chair of the 9/11 Commission, Thomas H. Kean, and Commissioners Richard Ben-Veniste, Bob Kerrey, Fred F. Fielding, John F. Lehman, Jamie S. Gorelick, Timothy J. Roemer, Slade Gorton, James R. Thompson and the entire 9/11 Commission staff for their bi-partisan commitment to ensuring that our nation takes the steps that are needed so that we do not endure another day like September 11, 2001.

Finally, I want to say a retrospective, comprehensive thank you to all of the teachers, professors, administrators, football and track coaches and staff from my elementary school, P.S. 251, my junior high school, J.H.S. 78, my high school, South Shore High School, all in Brooklyn, N.Y. and from my undergraduate alma mater, The University of Maryland, Eastern Shore and from my graduate alma mater, The Brooklyn Campus of Long Island University's School of Arts and Sciences, for all that you did to make me, *me*. You collectively joined together over the years with patience and passion to make sure that I read that book, completed that homework assignment, passed that test, went to class on time, did those push-ups, ran that sprint, finished that term paper and recited that speech. I am who I am because of your determination and commitment. May God bless all of you and thank you for being you!

Index

About the Author

Gregory Thomas is the Director of the Program for School Preparedness and Planning in the National Center for Disaster Preparedness at the Columbia University Mailman School of Public Health. He assists schools around the nation in the assessment and improvement of their current level of emergency preparedness. Thomas has co-authored three books on school safety for the Janes Information Group, including what has been called the most comprehensive book published to date on school safety, the *Janes Safe School Planning Guide for All Hazards.*

During his more than twenty years of public service, Thomas has served as the Executive Director of the Office of School Safety and Planning with the New York City Department of Education (during the terrorist attacks of September 11, 2001), Assistant Commissioner with the New York City Fire Department, Associate Director of the City University of New York/New York City Police Department Cadet Program at John Jay College of Criminal Justice, and a Senior Investigator and member of the executive staff with the Mollen Commission, the mayoral commission that investigated corruption within the New York City Police Department, and as a First Deputy Inspector General with the New York City Department of Investigation.

Born and raised in Brooklyn, New York, Gregory completed public school in New York City, and attended college at the University of Maryland, Eastern Shore where he received his Bachelor of Arts Degree in Sociology, and the Brooklyn Campus of Long Island University (L.I.U.) where he received his Master of Science Degree in Criminal Justice. Gregory currently resides with his family in Brooklyn, N.Y.